UP RODE THE TROOPERS

The Black Police in Queensland

Bill Rosser

University of Queensland Press

First published 1990 by University of Queensland Press
Box 42, St Lucia, Queensland 4067 Australia

Typeset by University of Queensland Press
Printed in Australia by The Book Printer, Melbourne

Distributed in the USA and Canada by
International Specialized Book Services, Inc.,
5602 N.E. Hassalo Street, Portland, Oregon 97213-3640

Cataloguing in Publication Data

National Library of Australia

Rosser, Bill, 1927– .
Up rode the troopers: the black police in Queensland.

Includes index.

1. Queensland Native Police Force. [2]. Aboriginal Australian police — Queensland — History. [2]. Aborigines, Australian — Queensland — Government relations. 3. Police — Queensland — History. I. Title.

363.2'09943

ISBN 0 7022 2224 0

Believe it or not, dedicating a book is not an easy task.

So many people added their particular contributions, without which, at the time, the book would not have moved beyond square one. For instance, there was the material from the various libraries such as the Oxley Library here in Brisbane, the Mitchell Library in Sydney, the Australian Institute of Aboriginal Studies in Canberra and, of course, the Queensland State Archives.

I must also give great credit to the Redcliffe Library; in particular librarians John Scott (for his conscientious efforts in obtaining some required research material) and Tracie Jones (for her courteous assistance). I thank you both.

But what of old Jack? My old cobber, "Cyclone" Jack. I will not write any more of him here; the reader will quickly find the story of that old bugger in this book.

So, old mate, I dedicate this book to you and if your story helps — even a little — to assist white society to understand the resentment which has been burning in the black man's soul for two hundred years, then all those hours we spent in the boiling sun, the dust and the flies out in the scrubs of Urandangie will not have been in vain.

Contents

Cyclone Jack, whose grandfather clashed with Lieutenant Wheeler's contingent of the Native Mounted Police Force. He escaped with his young son (Cyclone Jack's father) by scaling a tree, and watched as his tribe was slaughtered.

Introduction

> So long as laws shall exist which create Hells in the midst of civilisation; so long as men are degraded, women ruined and children afraid; so long as there shall be ignorance, poverty and wretchedness on this earth, stories such as this must be told.
>
> Victor Hugo, *Les Misérables*

This is a true story. Some people will find this difficult to believe, I know. Like all dispassionate historians, I deal strictly in facts and leave humbug to the politicians.

When I conceived the idea to write this book about the early days of the Queensland Native Police Force it never occurred to me that, during those years which saw the settling-in period, or the establishing of the pastoral industry, Aboriginal life was held so cheaply or that white settlers were so avaricious, callous and resolute in their hungry impatience to squat on the most fertile lands. In doing so they were guilty of heinous crimes toward their fellow creatures. Notwithstanding the fact that the usurpers were of good British stock, endowed with the principles of justice and fair play, it became quite obvious that such noble qualities had deserted them:

> There was but one law for them that they will ever respect — the bullet; the sole logic, the cock of the rifles.[1]

> I would as soon as shoot a blackfellow as a dog.[2]

The fact that Aborigines had been settled in Australia for at least forty thousand years meant not a whit to the squatters. Blacks were driven far from their tribal lands into areas frequented by opposing tribes, thereby causing conflict of a different kind.

Those blacks who took exception to the white man's actions and refused to leave their tribal homes were ruthlessly slaughtered in the most brutal manner. So efficient did their methods become that entire tribes were annihilated.

On 1 May 1861, a Select Committee on the Native Police Force was appointed to enquire into the Force and the Conditions of the Aborigines Generally. (Extracts from the *Minutes of Evidence* of this enquiry are included in this book. Only the details pertinent to its subject matter are recorded, for the purpose of verification and, occasionally, amplification.)

Evidence given by Captain John Coley during the enquiry gives an insight into the treatment of Aborigines. Coley is being questioned by the Chairman:

Q. How long had the district been opened for settlement?
A. About twelve months.

Q. You have seen a good deal of the Aborigines since your arrival?
A. Yes.

Q. You tell the Committee of your own knowledge of what the number was on your arrival, that they have diminished since the settlement of the district?
A. Quite so. They are all gone, *altogether extinct*.

Q. In what way?
A. By *shooting* and *poisoning* them.

Q. What with?
A. *With strychnine and arsenic, in flour.*[3]

The methods of extermination varied as a matter of expediency. If the recalcitrant black could be caught, he would be summarily hanged.[4] If too fleet of foot, the unfortunate creatures would be shot mid-stride. But the most diabolic method of extermination was the practice of mixing arsenic with flour, which the blacks stole — as was intended — in order to supplement their fast-diminishing natural food supply, or which was presented to them as a "Christian act of kindness".

Unknown numbers perished in this manner. Another "act of kindness" was the fencing of various waterholes, ostensibly to keep out stock, thus assuring the blacks of an ample supply of unpolluted water. Aborigines initially appreciated this gesture until it became tragically apparent that the wily squatter had poisoned their waterhole! No form of redress was available to them; spears were no match for guns or the silvery-white powder.

So in response, the blacks carried out raids at night, a method of reprisal which frustrated the settlers as the raiders, like the Arabs of old, "disappeared into the night".

The dispossession of tribal land was not the only subject of contention between black and white. Settlers, their employees and many of the young bloods were partial to the young Aboriginal women — crudely referred to as "black velvet". Most of these women, regardless of age, were already betrothed to members of their ilk; violation of these customs was looked upon — and treated — as a very serious offence and dealt with harshly.[5] The Hornet Bank Station massacre in 1857 was the direct result of such widespread violations, but more about that later.

Thus it was, in the early days of settlement; owing to white man's rape, kidnapping, chicanery and the destruction of Aboriginal life, Aborigines altered from a race of friendly, harmless people to a suspicious misanthropic people. Because of these tribal violations, blacks reacted as one might expect. In order to protect their families and to retain as much of their tribal lands as possible, they were forced into open conflict — it was no longer enough to spear cattle and rob huts.

To combat the marauding blacks in south-east Queensland, a contingent of Native Mounted Police — the Troopers — was established in the Condamine and Burnett districts for the protection of squatters. Later, as a result of attacks on the Dowse family near the coast, the Headquarters was established at Sandgate, a small settlement to the north of Brisbane. Recruits who were to be employed as troopers were brought great distances, some from over six hundred kilometres away. The reasoning behind this was that these distant tribesmen were the natural enemies of the local blacks and therefore would have no compunction in killing them. The promise of an inexhaustible supply of women, their food supplied and the opportunity to attack hostile tribes with superior arms induced an ample supply of recruits. (The promise of food fell somewhat flat because, more often than not, the troopers were forced to feed their white officers with bush tucker as not enough provisions could be carried on some of their more lengthy excursions in their pursuit of "worrisome" blacks.) Led by white officers, and equipped with horses, authority and guns, this band of murderous little bastards was the perfect killing machine! Training was perfunctory and, provided a recruit was able to walk a straight line and place the correct end of a gun to his shoulder, their training was considered to be adequate. Their pay consisted of about one pound per month. They were provided with a uniform of sorts — which they discarded most of the time. Their weapons were usually smooth bore guns which, with a missile about the size of a thumb, turned a man into mince-meat! The officers of the force wore revolvers and swords; the latter were used with great effect whenever blacks were "dispersed" at close quarters.[6]

The Native Police Force was established in 1848 and Lieutenant Frederick Walker, an ex-station manager, was appointed as Commandant. Walker had a somewhat chequered career in the Force although it cannot be denied that he terrified the blacks! But he liked the bottle and it became his downfall; on 19 January 1855, he was dismissed from the Force for constantly being in a state of inebriation.[7] After his dismissal, Walker formed his own private corps of mounted police, taking some of his former troopers with him. The government, however, deemed it an illegal force and ordered Walker to disband it. Later, on 7 September 1861, he led an expedition from Rockhampton in search of the missing explorers, Burke and Wills. He died at Floraville, in the Gulf country, on 19 November 1866.[8]

As the result of conscientious efforts exerted by some zealous squatters and the Native Police — led by their equally zealous white officers — Aboriginal numbers quickly fell. Anthropologists now estimate that, in 1800, the black population was 750,000. Fifty years later the number had fallen to around 55,000 and the race seemed to be heading for ultimate destruction.[9] Some sensationalist scribes have claimed that the Aborigines were cannibalistic and were literally *eating each other out of existence*, an absurdity which is not worthy of further mention in these pages. Though absurd, such claims did earn Aboriginal society considerable obloquy for a time.

Throughout the years it has very often been claimed that Aborigines *were* cannibals. I have heard people state that Aborigines were in the habit of killing or "sacrificing" fat young babies and gins for culinary purposes. This popular fallacy was bandied around by white racists ignorant of Aboriginal customs and tradition. I do not deny that blacks ate human flesh, but it was a practice not dissimilar to the white paganistic ritual of partaking of the "flesh and blood" of Jesus Christ!

Perhaps it would mean more to the reader if I repeat a passage from Constance Petrie's book about her father, *Tom Petrie's Reminiscences of Early Queensland*. It is undeniable that Petrie's knowledge of the Queensland Aborigine, that is to say, within a considerable area in south east Queensland, far exceeded that of his contemporaries. He was fluent in five languages and their dialects, and had grown up with blacks since early childhood. Constance Petrie writes:

> My father says there is no truth in this statement;[10] it is just hearsay, as there was no such thing as sacrifice among the Queensland Aborigines, neither did they ever kill any one for the purpose of eating them . . . however . . . they always ate a man noted for his fighting abilities, or a *turrwan* (great man). First, the body was carried about a mile away from camp. A *turrwan* would take a piece of dry sapwood from an old tree, and lighting it well by the fire, would keep knocking off the red ashes till it burnt with a flame like a candle. With this he would

give the body an extra good singeing all over, excepting the head, until the skin turned from black to a light brown colour . . . three or four men . . . would slowly advance, one by one, singing a certain tune, to the body. Each of these men held a shell or stone knife in his hand. The first would start by slitting the skin open from the head down the neck, then retiring; his place would be taken by the second man, who would carry the opening down the body, the third man down the legs, and so on till the skin was opened right to the heels, and would peel off in one whole piece. During this performance never a joke or a laugh was heard, but everything was carried out with the utmost quietude and solemnity. The whole tribe, sitting around in groups . . . each possessing a fire . . . as the old men divided out the flesh in pieces to each lot.[11]

It was the common practice to then, after drying, place the skin and bones in a "dilly" to be carried around by a female relative. When this relative became tired of carrying it about it would be placed in the hollow of a tree or in a cave.

The loss of more than ninety per cent of Aborigines in fifty years was never officially explained. It was incumbent on the Native Police officers to record and report on the number of fatalities caused by their operations, but this was not done — not even approximately. No records of "dispersals", as they were known, were kept. An ex-officer of the Native Police Force wrote:

> As I served in the Force during a portion of the early sixties, I will endeavour to describe as accurately as possible the sort of life we led . . . At the same time it will be obvious to any Queenslander of those days that some episodes connected with the doings of the Force cannot be published.[12]

Perhaps the most sadistic and merciless officer in the Queensland Native Police Force was Lieutenant Frederick Wheeler. He was appointed Second Lieutenant on 7 December 1857, and during the latter part of his career he was attached to the Sandgate Headquarters. It was this officer who shot and crippled the grandfather of my friend, Cyclone Jack, with whom I have spent many hours in the hot, dusty, fly-infested little township of Urandangie, and whose story provided the impetus for this book. This collection of small buildings was more or less considered "home" to the remnants of the Warluwara tribe. They still live "the old way" in most respects although, I fancy, many a goanna or kangaroo owes its longevity to the regular arrival of Social Security cheques.

It was Wheeler's tenet that "all must die — the innocent with the guilty". The manner in which he phrased his reports was of quite some concern to the Colonial Secretary. He pointed out that he could not permit an impression *back in England* that "wholesale slaughter of Aborigines was to be committed *under authority*".[13] Lieutenant Wheeler subsequently retracted his statement that "the innocent must suffer for the guilty", explaining to the Government Resident, Wickham, that he never intended to act out this expression.[14] Of course, history has proved that he did, indeed, "act out this expression", using the two chief ingredients which made up the essential quality of his nature — cruelty and zeal. Another officer of the force, Lieutenant John O'Connell Bligh, possessed similar qualities. Bligh became Commandant of the Force after Morisset retired.[15]

Yet another cause of Aboriginal deaths on a large scale was the introduction of venereal disease. This was brought to the government's notice in 1897 (though not for the first time):

> A very silly yet general impression exists among some ignorant bushmen that when suffering from gonorrhea all they need do is impart the disease to some female, then the severity of such

> disease upon themselves will be greatly modified, or perhaps totally cured. Can you imagine anything so heinous? It [sic] have seen poor gins, merely children between 11 and 14 years of age, suffering from syphilis in all its stages.[16]

As Aborigines confronted the widespread destruction of their race during these early days of white settlement, a few faced a different kind of dilemma. During the proceedings of the 1861 Select Committee, Reverend Ridley, whose task it was to "civilise" the blacks, reported on the success of one of his charges, an Aborigine called Bungaree:

> Bungaree who, after taking prizes in Sydney College speaking good Latin and behaving as a gentleman in elegant society, returned to the bush and, in 1852, he entered the Black Police. He once said to Lieutenant Fulford in a melancholy tone (who repeated the remark to me at Surat on the Condamine) "I wish I had never been taken out of the bush, and educated as I have been for I cannot be a white man — they will never look on me as one of themselves; and I cannot be a blackfellow — I am disgusted with their way of living."[17]

Bungaree became "assimilated" into white society but did he do well? When he died at Traylan on 21 July 1854, he was still a young man. As far as blacks "doing well" is concerned, consider this:

> Neither government action, nor the law, nor public opinion need obstruct the pursuit of profit. If necessary, resident blacks could be expelled from their traditional lands, murdered and enslaved if they were needed for labour or sex.[18]

As previously stated, in 1861 a Select Committee was established to enquire into the Native Police Force. But, as soon as the Committee members' names were announced, the enquiry came under attack. The Committee was "stacked", claimed knowing people. The black ink of the presses took on a darker hue! "Shame", said some people. "Conniving at corruption", said others. Newspaper articles and letters to the editor abounded:

> Again the Government have set about stifling an honest enquiry into the mis-doings of this disgraceful force, and absolutely "packed" a committee of the house to effect their object. Before your leader was seen in this quarter, all to whom I spoke about the creation of that committee, agreed that once more a wicked farce was to be perpetrated in the name of her Majesty's Ministers — again a piece of jobbery was to be carried on — for the sake of pleasing government supporters in the House, and of hiding the intentional past blindness of [Governor] Sir George Bowen. Shame! Shame! [19]

Some of the questions asked of witnesses by members of the Committee were barely credible. In many instances, not only were the questions asked, but the answers were provided also — in the same sentence. Probably the most consistent offender was Chairman MacKenzie. His questioning of Sneyd (himself an ex-sergeant of the Force of some seventeen years standing) was proof enough of the desired result of the enquiry. His questions to Sneyd on the Myall Creek massacre (see p.178) provide textbook examples of judicial bias. Sneyd, of course, knew it all. What he did not know, MacKenzie told him:

> Q. *Was it not the case* that a number of whites — comrades of these men who were executed — had been murdered?
>
> Q. *Are you aware* that they were convicted on *circumstantial evidence?*
>
> Q. Is it not the case that the blacks broke out upon the Namoi again, and that a large detachment of police was sent down, after this *judicial murder, for I can call it nothing else?* [20]

The enquiry came to an end in July 1861, and the report was published on 17 July. The enquiry, as many people had predicted, was an absolute sham. One officer, Lieutenant John Murray, was dismissed from the force. And yet by comparison, Murray's "crime" was in no way as serious as those committed by Bligh, Wheeler and many of the squatters. All Murray had been guilty of was handing his detachment of troopers over — temporarily — to a junior officer. But the detachment, under the junior officer, killed some blacks. Nothing new in that; nobody had seemed to worry about killing blacks before. But in this case the junior officer just happened to be Commandant Morisset's young brother. Moreover, the owner of the station on which the blacks had been killed, John Mortimer, was kicking up a fuss about it. He complained to the newspapers about the massacre. He went so far as to insert a two-column expose by way of an advertisement in the *Moreton Bay Courier*. (This drew a quick response from the Colonial Secretary, seeking full information about the affair. Mortimer replied, explaining all the gory details.) However, the final solution was that, rather than have young Rudolph Morisset stigmatised, Murray "would have to go". Actually, the claim — or suggestion — put to various witnesses that second Lieutenant Rudolph Morisset was "new to the Force and inexperienced in his duties" was yet another attempt at exoneration of young Morisset. One witness, Charles F.D. Parkinson, was asked by a member of the Committee: "Do you think it right or proper that a young and inexperienced officer like Mr Morisset should be placed in charge of a detachment of Police?" Parkinson replied: "He has had more experience than many other young men who have been appointed to the Force."[21]

Perhaps the main reason why Murray should not have been scapegoated out of the Force was provided by the evidence of Commandant Morisset *himself* when the Chairman asked him for his opinion of young

Morisset's suitability and efficiency as an officer: "I again ask — do you think that a young officer should be entrusted with a detachment, and go blazing away into the blacks in that way?" Morisset replied: "I don't know that he should go blazing away into the blacks, but *his former experience was quite enough to entitle him to take charge of a detachment* in any case."[22] Earlier, when questioned about Rudolph Morisset's ability and capability with a detachment, Commandant Morisset had answered in his brother's favour. When the Committee Chairman asked: "Do you not think it improper to entrust such a young officer with the charge of a detachment, in such a case as this?", Commandant Morisset replied: "*I don't think so*, because, although Lieutenant Morisset had not been long in the Force, *he had had as much experience with the Native Police Force as many of the officers.*"[23]

There are two further instances regarding the massacre on Mortimer's station which do not ring true. Both are unfavourable to Second Lieutenant Morisset. In his report to the Colonial Secretary, he states: ". . . on two or three occasions I found it necessary to fire upon them before they would disperse."[24] Also, in evidence given by Charles F.D. Parkinson, it is stated that a black boy who was with the police on Mortimer's station "fired both barrels of his gun" at the blacks who then retaliated by throwing spears and nulla-nullas; the police were *then* obliged to fire at them.[25] Both the foregoing attestations were in direct contrast to the Chairman's remarks in his report which is given in full on p.199.

It would appear that Lieutenant John Ross, the patsy for the Hornet Bank affair, was not the only scapegoat of the Native Police Force. The Committee further justified its decision to dismiss Murray by letting it be known that he drank liquor. Who didn't? It was pretty common knowledge that officers supplied their troopers with alcohol.

The report, and the Committee members' discourse about it, was treated with contempt by most citizens and, on even a cursory glance through its pages, it is soon apparent that it is a document of exoneration rather than one of investigation. In part, the Committee Report states:

> Lieutenant Wheeler appears to have acted with indiscretion on his late visit to the Logan and Fassifern. Your Committee recommend that he should be reprimanded, and removed to another district: were it not that in other respects he is a most valuable and zealous Officer, they would feel it their duty to recommend his dismissal.
>
> With respect to the affray at Mr Mortimer's, it appears that the detachment of police stationed at Maryborough was most improperly handed over by the Officer in charge, Lieutenant Murray, to Second Lieutenant Morisset, a young officer newly appointed, unacquainted with his duties, and also with the Troopers placed under his control . . . After a careful consideration of the evidence in this case, your Committee recommend that Lieutenant Murray should be removed from the Force, both on this account, and his general unfitness for his duties . . .
>
> The evidence taken by your Committee shews beyond doubt that all attempts to Christianize or educate the Aborigines of Australia have hitherto proved abortive. . . Credible witnesses shew that they are *addicted to cannibalism* . . . and are *sunk in the lowest depths of barbarism.*[26]

The severing of black fingers for use as pipe rammers; the staking of decapitated black heads on gate-posts and the chopping up of helpless black men, women and children with cutlasses were acts which sank even lower than the "lowest depths of barbarism" and one wonders if the Sons of England had the necessary qualifications to "*Christianize*" and "*educate*" the Aborigines of Australia!

"They used to flog me with a whip"

The grey light of dawn was brightening in the east as I urged my vehicle onward towards Dajarra, a small cattle town in western Queensland. I had purposely driven throughout the night with the hope of catching sight of the renowned Min-min lights which are reputed to be seen as ghostly pools of lights dancing across the paddocks and along the sides of the road between Winton and Boulia. I had stopped many times — eyes straining and neck hair creeping — trying to spot the phenomenon but without success.

It was about 7.00 a.m. when I finally reached Boulia. I decided to break my journey to say hello to one of my friends, Peggy James, with whom I had spent many hours during a previous visit, recording her life story.[1] As I was turning into the main street I noticed an elderly Aborigine walking along the road, headed towards a group of huts which were situated further up the street. I came up beside him and spoke to him. He was a friendly man as, indeed, are most of the people in this part of the country. After a short chat he invited me to his home. (A huge machine shed, with concrete floor and meagre furnishing, it was nevertheless quite comfortable.) He was probably in his late seventies yet he walked briskly and held himself erect. He wore a neatly creased pair of brown slacks and a white shirt which was tucked roughly into the waist. Deep creases dissected a large face and his eyes were black and piercing below a deeply furrowed brow. His hair was surprisingly thick and, of course, very grey and he wore sideburns almost down to his chin. His feet were bare. His name was Jimmy Larkin.

When we arrived inside his house he waved me to a chair. He spoke clear English yet with a trace of "lingo". When an Aborigine speaks "lingo" (which is of course a common nickname for "language") he speaks either broken English or his own tribal language. Sometimes, if he gets excited enough, he mixes all three. I explained to Jimmy that I was interested in Aboriginal history and he nodded his head in understanding. He assured me that he would be only too willing to assist me in any way he could. We finished with the small talk and we were soon in serious conversation. I asked him if he had any objection to my using a tape recorder.

"No," he smiled. "I've had one of those things for years." He held out his tobacco tin, offering me one of his smokes. Like most of the stockmen to whom I have spoken in the bush, he was an exceedingly friendly man and, of course, he had spent most of his working life as a stockman.

"How much were you paid as a stockman, Jimmy?" I asked. I fancied I already knew the answer but it was a standard question which I had to ask.

"They don't give you any pay," he replied, smiling at my apparent ignorance. I noticed for the first time that he had several teeth missing.

"Did you know anything about money in those days?" He spat his well-chewed cigarette butt onto the ground before answering.

"No, I knew nothing about money," he said. "Still don't know. All I know is that it don't go far. A couple of packets of smokes and a bit of bread and it's all gone again." He gave a disgusted look and began rolling another cigarette.

"No," he repeated. "They didn't give me any money."

"Well, then, Jimmy, what did they give you in return for your work?" He thought for a while and scratched his snowy hair.

"Aw, clothes and stuff," he replied. "That's all they'd give you in those days. Not much." He interlocked his fingers and placed them on top of his head. "Oh, well," he continued. "They used to give us something for the races sometimes. They'd give me a few bob to spend.[2] I don't know how much they gave me. They gave me lollies. Lollies and fruit." He laughed at the memory.

"Where did they hold the race meetings, Jimmy?"

"At a place called Rankin."

"Was that the name of a station?"

"No, it was a little bush town. It had a pub and a store."

"Did you ever drink at the pub?" I asked, handing him back his tobacco tin.

"No, no," he replied quickly.

"Why not?" I asked.

"We wasn't allowed to drink. Only white people were allowed to drink. We couldn't because we were under the Act."[3]

"Oh," I remarked. "You knew about the Act?"

"Yes, I knew about it. They wouldn't allow us to drink. They had it here in Boulia for a long time, too. We couldn't get a drink anywhere."

"How else did the Act affect you, Jimmy?"

He uncoupled his hands and rubbed his chin thoughtfully.

"Well," he said, after a little while. "We had to work on the cattle stations but they had to feed us when we had a holiday." He noticed my frown. "We had rations, you know," he explained. "They had to feed us to keep us there. We'd be there when the work started, you know. They used to give us tents to live in."

"Could you leave the job if you wanted to?" I asked.

"Yes," he answered. "You could leave but you had to be back when the work started. He's your boss. That's your job there now." [4]

"Did the boss give you enough tucker or did you have to hunt for some of your food?" I enquired.

"Well," he answered matter-of-factly. "We were far out in the bush, see. When we ran out of tucker we had to hunt for the bush tucker, you know. The wild tucker. Kangaroo meat. Emu. Whatever you could get." He gave an infectious laugh as he spoke about hunting.

I formed the opinion that hunting to him, now, would be somewhat of a joke. His lifestyle had changed. The rifle now supplants the spear. The coolamon is out and the plastic bucket is in. Country and western music played on a battery-operated tape recorder excites him now as once, perhaps, only the sonant sobbing of the didgeridoo and the corroboree could.

"We used to get plenty of honey, too," Jimmy was saying. "Wild honey from the trees."

"How did you get that, Jimmy?"

"We used to cut down the trees and cut the honey out." He made slashing movements with his hands.

"How did you keep the honey?"

"Oh, we used a piece of bark to keep it in. We had no

billy cans in those days. We used to get a piece of bark with a dip in it. Coolamon, that was what we called it. There was plenty of fruit there, too."

"What sort of fruit was there, Jimmy?"

"Wild blackberry."

"Plum? Wild plum?"

"Yes, plenty of plum."

"What about chinky-apple. Any of those?" His eyes lit up as he thought about the small, apple-shaped fruit which grows on an extremely prickly bush.

"Oh, yes," he replied. "Big trees of them. They still there. Down around Charters Towers and places like that. Plenty of yams, too. There were two sorts of them."

"Did you take the lot or did you leave some to grow bigger?"

"We took the lot," Jimmy replied. "We would take whatever was there. Plenty more would come. There were vines everywhere. The women would get them and carry them home."

"Plenty of bush tucker, was there?"

"Oh, stacks," he responded. "Not much animal though. Those station blokes hunted them all away. We used to get a lot of grass seeds, too. There was pepper-grass and seeds from what they call Nardoo. Then there was pigweed seed. The women would get it all up and grind it up fine. You could eat it like that or you could make a kind of damper and put it in the coals."

"Would it be good to go back to those days, Jimmy?" I asked. "Would you like to go and live the wild life again?"

He moved to a chair and sat down, pondering my question. He broke out in a slow grin.

"Aw," he said. "It would be hard now."

"Why do you say that, Jimmy? Why would it be hard?"

"Well," he explained. "It would be hard to hunt, you know. It would be hard to get something to eat. Goanna. Kangaroo. You got to go a long way now. It's not like it used to be. You got to get in a truck now."

"It's easier to get them with a rifle, is it?"

"Aw, yes," Jimmy said coyly. "It's better with the rifle. Shoot kangaroo. Better than shooting bullocks, you know. You get in jail." He gave out with that melodious laugh again as he finished speaking.

"What about some of those blackfellas still out there in the bush. Do they still kill bullocks?" Jimmy was not sure how to answer my question. He looked at me cautiously before replying.

"Aw, they reckon they used to do it one time. The Walgra tribe used to do it. But not now, I think."

"Were the Walgra tribe a friendly mob? Were they friendly with your tribe?"

"By gee, I don't think so. They won't fight but they don't mix much. That's a different tribe. Talk different language."

"Could one of the boys from your tribe marry a girl from their tribe?" Jimmy shook his head vigorously and looked at me with alarm.

"No," he said hurriedly. "Not allowed. They mightn't like a strange girl. No, that would not be allowed. But it's a bit different now, I suppose."

"Supposing," I persisted, "a girl and a boy from your tribe ran away together without getting married. What would happen?"

"Oh, well," he pressed his chin into his chest. "There would be big trouble over that."

"What would happen?"

"Well," he explained, "the girl would get killed. Or the man. One of them has to go."

"How would that happen? How would they kill them?"

Jimmy remained silent for a moment, scratching his cheek with a forefinger. He licked his lips and frowned.

"Well," he answered, hesitantly, "we don't know. They have their own secret ways. We never ask them questions either."

"Who decided which one of the two was to die? Who made the decision about these things?"

"Oh, all the people. They have a meeting and they decide because the boy and the girl done wrong. They run away."

"And, Jimmy," I pressed on, "suppose a girl from your tribe and a boy from another tribe ran away. What would happen?"

"One of them has to go. The boy or the girl." He looked at me and shook his head slightly. "It's hard, isn't it," he remarked.

It appeared obvious to me that Jimmy was not at all anxious to continue this line of discussion. A change of subject was required. I remembered that he had told me previously that he had spent most of his younger life in the Northern Territory.

"Why did you come to Queensland, Jimmy? Did you come here because of your work?" He shuffled his feet over the floor as he collected his thoughts.

"Well, as a matter of fact," he replied, "I came here because they were too bloody rough in the Territory."

"What do you mean, 'rough'?"

"Well, they used to flog you up there." He winced slightly as he spoke. "They used to tie them to a tree with a chain. That's why I cleared out of there. It was just too bloody rough." The thin line of Jimmy's compressed lips told me he was recalling unpleasant events from the past.

"Did they flog you?" I asked him.

"Yes." He jutted his face towards me. "They used to flog me with a whip across the back."

"Why did they flog you?"

"To put sense into you."

"What do you mean?"

"They reckon they flog you so you know not to do anything wrong. That's their idea in the Territory. They want to frighten you so you won't be cheeky, or something like that. See, you've got to do what you're told. You've got to do what the white people tell you to do."

"That's a savage way to frighten you, isn't it?" I remarked.

He gave a side-of-the-mouth grin.

"That's true," he agreed.

"What would happen if you hit the white bloke back?"

"Well," he gave a half laugh, "there might be two or three on to you then and they'd bash you up?"

"The three of them would get stuck into you?"

"Yes. You can't get a win anywhere. You've just got to take what's coming to you." Jimmy's eyes narrowed before continuing.

"I remember one time out on Eva Downs station. This bloke was flogging this married couple that worked on the station. I don't know what they done. They wanted to get back to Tennant Creek station, see. They took off one morning from where they were camped and when the boss got up in the morning he found that they were gone. They went walking to Tennant Creek. The boss got on his horse and he had his revolver and his stockwhip with him. He caught up to the married couple and flogged them all the way back and then he sacked them." Jimmy unconsciously drew his shoulder blades together as if feeling the lash before continuing.

"Somebody reported it and they took him to Darwin Court for flogging with his whip. He made a big mark on the wife's back. It cost the boss about four hundred dollars fine."

"Did they confiscate the bastard's whip?" I asked.

"Yes," Jimmy replied. "The police came out there. They took his whip away from him. That's what they used to do, you know. It was pretty rough. That's why I got out of the Territory."

Jimmy sat in silence, rolling a thin cigarette. The tobacco was dry and it crumbled to dust as he began rolling it. He lit it and blew a cloud of blue smoke into the air. I did not interrupt his thoughts. I eyed him closely as he picked flecks of tobacco from his tongue. Suddenly he sat upright and turned to me.

"You know what," he said, fiercely. "The police caught up with us and wanted to know how many people were here from the Territory. They wanted us to go back to our own land."

"Would you go back, Jimmy?" I asked.

"Gee, I don't know." He inclined his head sideways. "I reckon it would be more better down here. That land up there is all desert country, you know. I wouldn't know my way around there now. I used to when I was young, but not now."

"What Dreaming are you, Jimmy?" He had to think fairly hard for a while before his eyes lit up.

"Ah," he said. "Snake. I'm Snake Dreaming. Carpet Snake. I got a name for it but I wouldn't know it now. My mother was Emu Dreaming. You know Jack

Punch?"[5] I nodded. "Well, he's cousin-brother [half-brother]. Another old bloke up there at Dajarra, old George Nemo, he's a cousin-brother, too." He smiled as he thought of his last sighting of old George Nemo.

"He's this one," he said, holding an imaginary bottle to his lips.

"Don't tell me he's like that," I said with amusement.

"He must be after the young sheilas." Jimmy gave that musical laugh again and I found myself wanting to hear his laugh more.

"What sort of work do you do now, Jimmy?" I enquired. He shrugged his shoulders before replying.

"I don't do any work at all now. I'm pensioned off."

"Which station did you work on when you were a drover?"

"I wasn't working for any station," he told me. "I used to take cattle from the out-stations and drove them to the meatworks."

As we spoke, some of Jimmy's friends came along, seeking his company to go fishing at the river. He rose and brushed his cigarette ash from his clothes.

"I'd like to see you again," he said as he shook my hand. "These blokes want me to go with them so I'd better go." He turned to his companions and said, "If I don't go, you mob would get lost." They all laughed at Jimmy's facetiousness. We said our goodbyes and, as he walked slowly up the road, I made a mental note. "Yes. I'll certainly see you again when I return to this area."

I entered my vehicle and headed towards the house where my friend, Peggy James, lived. On arrival I was informed that Peggy was having a few days in Mt Isa and would not be returning until the weekend. With nothing more to keep me in Boulia, I drove out of the town and headed for Dajarra.

"I had a good run, Ruby," I smiled at my old friend. "There were not too many kangaroos on the road. You've just about got them all cleaned up for your dogs."[7] She nodded in mock disgust at my banter.

"You must admit, though," she said, pointing to the three mongrel dogs which were curled up in front of the fire, "they're pretty fat, aren't they?" I nodded in agreement.

As Ruby walked towards the house I noticed a pronounced limp.

"What's wrong with your leg, Ruby?" I enquired. She raised the hem of her dress modestly to expose a badly swollen knee.

"It's arthritis," she groaned. Her expression changed from one of concern to one of contempt.

"Doctors!" she huffed. "I don't know. One bloke tells me I've got arthritis. I go to another doctor and he tells me I've got arthritis. I say to them, 'What's this. Is that the password of something?' One bloke tells me to take this tablet and the other bloke tells me they're no good and gives me another one. I don't know which is the right bottle half the time."

I looked closely at her. Her hands, which had reined many an unruly horse and had headed many recalcitrant bullocks on her droving stints were now knobbly and crooked. The four fingers of her right hand slanted sideways and her thumb formed the letter "C". However, her painful affliction had not suppressed the impish gleam in her eyes nor her contented disposition.

"Anyway," she continued, as she poked several sticks into the fire, "how long are you up for?"

I gave her question considerable thought. I really had not planned on a particular time limit. I was here simply until my cash ran out.

"Well, Ruby," I replied, "if you remember, when I

spoke to you on the phone the other day I mentioned that I would like to go out to Urandangie. At the time, you said you would like to go also. Do you still want to go?" She looked up quickly from the fire.

"Too right, I'd like to," she said eagerly. "When do you want to go? I'm ready any time." She waved her hand towards the others.

"These jokers can look after themselves. They'll be all right."

"I'd like to go as soon as possible," I replied. Ruby turned the palms of her hands upwards in a gesture of submission.

"Oh, well. We could go on Monday," she suggested.

"That would be really good," I assured her.

While we had been talking, Ruby's niece, Glenda, had made a big billy of tea. I couldn't remember when tea tasted so good. I could feel the red dust being washed from my throat. As we sipped our tea I noticed for the first time that Harry had two fingers missing from his left hand. He noticed my gaze and, understanding my curiosity, he held up the mutilated hand.

"Lost 'em shoein' 'orses," he explained laconically. "These fingers went with the 'orse."

"How long ago was that, Harry?" I asked.

"It 'appened in 1974," he replied, looking down at the stumps. He dismissed the subject with a smile.

As Harry finished speaking, someone started strumming a guitar next door. We looked across and saw a group of youths in the yard tuning up for a "singsong". They were a happy bunch of young men, active and full of life. Presently they broke out into full song. The strains of "Cottonfields" drifted across the township. I could not resist taking my tape recorder across in order to capture their merriment. After returning to my friends at the fire, I overheard Ruby mention something about fishing. I enquired about this.

"Oh," Ruby replied. "I was just saying that we might catch a few fish on the Diamantina while you are here." I looked quizzically at her for a moment, ever wary of Ruby's leg-pulling.

"Sure," I said, facetiously. "The fish are there in their thousands, aren't they?" Ruby over-emphasised a sniff.

"Oh, no. There's not that many," she replied stiffly. "But the fact is, when you go fishing on the Diamantina, you've got to hide behind a tree to bait your hook otherwise the fish will chase you for it!" I might have known. We all laughed at her joke. Despite her painful arthritis, Ruby had still retained her capacity for wit.

"Oh, well," I replied, innocently. "We'll see."

Harry Spencer rolled his cigarette around his mouth with prehensile lips.

"By the way, Bill," he asked. "Where are you going to sleep tonight?" His question took me by surprise because I had not considered this. After some thought I shrugged my shoulders in defeat.

"In my truck, I suppose," I replied. "I've slept in it a good many times and had a reasonable night's sleep."

"Aw, be buggered," Harry spat his cigarette butt into the fire. "I've got a spare bed upstairs at my place. Stay there."

However comfortable the truck was, sleeping in a bed would be much warmer.

"Thanks, Harry," I smiled. "I'll take you up on that. I've got my sleeping bag with me so I won't need blankets. I'll move up after I've had some more of this tea." That problem now settled, I mentioned my proposed trip to Urandangie again. Jack Punch, who was nodding off in the warm glow of the log fire, opened his eyes and looked over to me.

"Bill," he said, sleepily. "I'd like to go with you too. I speak the lingo so I might be a bit of a help."

His words were music to my ears. In the past I have sometimes had difficulty in collecting valuable oral histories from very old tribal people whose language is heavy with lingo. Jack would be invaluable to me.

"You're on," I said, eagerly. "I was wondering how I was going to get over that language problem. You've solved it in one hit." Jack gave a smile which appeared to be gratitude but I was the grateful one.

"Reckon you could leave on Monday?"

"Aw, yes. No problem," he drawled.

It was getting late now, almost eleven o'clock. The fire had died to glowing embers and talk had decreased to just a few grunted remarks. I felt tired as the last twenty-four hours had been a pretty long grind.

I said goodnight and, collecting my sleeping bag, slouched off to Harry's spare bed.

It was Friday the thirteenth.

"Only tents and bough sheds"

I rose early on Saturday morning to a beautiful day. A gentle breeze was blowing and the tips of the tallest gums, still wet with dew, took on the appearance of gold-plated sequins as they danced in the early morning sun. I sought out Jack to help him prepare for our sojourn in Urandangie. I was unable to locate him so I asked around. During the night he had had to make a hurried trip to Mt Isa with his son and was not expected to return until the following Wednesday. So, "the best-laid plans of mice and men", et cetera.

To make matters worse, Ruby was feeling ill. Whilst at Mt Isa she had eaten a meal which included tomatoes, and Ruby's reaction to tomatoes causes her to be cautious about straying too far from the necessary facility. So, I was all dressed up with nowhere to go, so to speak.

"I'm sorry about this," Ruby apologised. A tincture of sadness showed in her face. "I'll take some more of this muck and see how I feel." She held up a bottle which contained a thick whitish liquid. She turned and disappeared into the house.

So as not to disturb her I crossed the yard to Harry's place. Gladys, Harry's wife, was busily sweeping the back steps. She was a big, friendly woman. Perhaps the loose, full-skirted dress which she wore accentuated her size. Her hair was jet black and it turned in a shallow wave at the ends. Her genial face, deeply creased on each side of her cheeks and dabbed with a round pudgy nose, seemed to be set in a permanent smile, exposing a full set of white, even teeth. Two dark, warm eyes peering out from beneath bushy eyebrows completed her countenance.

"My word," she remarked as I approached. "It's getting hot."

"You're not wrong," I responded. "I must be mad for wanting to go to Urandangie. They reckon it's worse out there."

She smiled at my remarks.

"It'll be hot out there all right," she warned. "I know what the heat is like out there." She puffed out her cheeks to emphasise her words. She finished sweeping and stowed the broom between the washing machine and the steps. She invited me upstairs out of the heat and, after she had washed her hands, we both sat at the kitchen table.

"Were you born at Urandangie, Gladys?" I asked her.

"No, I was born at Mt Isa but I've been here all my life."

"Here, in Dajarra?"

"Yes, all my life." She was looking idly at a book which lay upon the table. I wondered if, in fact, she could read. I knew she had been to school. Ruby had told me that.

"Gladys, can you read?" I asked her.

"Oh, yes," she replied, taking up the book. "I read fairly well."

"Can you write, also?"

"Mmm, yes. I can write."

"Where did you go to school, Gladys?"

"Here, in Dajarra," she replied. "I went to school here." She pointed in the direction of the school which was in the next street. It occurred to me that, if Gladys had spent all her life here, she would be able to tell me a great deal about the town's history.

"When you were younger, when you first came here, where did you live?" She looked at the floor, sending her mind back to those early days.

"Just across the creek," she pointed with her chin to a small creek which lay at the lower end of the town. "That was the main camp," she explained. "It was called West End. It was the western part of town."

"There wouldn't have been many houses around in those days, would there?"

"No," she smiled tolerantly. "Only tents and bough-sheds. That's all we had."

"How many Aboriginal kids went to school here?"

"Oh, quite a few." She nodded towards a small brown building up near the post office. It was a very ancient structure. "That was the school there then. It was the first school. There was just the school and bough-sheds then. That's all we had."

"Did you work on cattle stations when you grew up?"

"Yes. I left school when I was fourteen and the first place I worked was at Carandotta station."

"Were you there when Ruby De Satge was there?"

"No, not really," Gladys replied. "I only saw her when she used to come through on droving trips."

"What sort of work did you do on the stations?"

"I was a housemaid." She put a hand over her mouth to conceal an embarrassed smile. "Once, there was a lot of housemaids but you don't see many these days."

"No," I agreed. "They're scarce now, all right. Tell me, Gladys, were they good people to work for?"

"Oh, yes," she said. "They were all right, I suppose."

"Who were they? Do you remember the boss's name?"

"Yes. It was Mawl. The manager was Ted Mawl in those days. He was there a long time."

"Did they give you any pay?" She half closed her eyes at the question.

"Yes, they used to pay me but the money went straight to the police station in those days."

"Of course," I explained. "That was because of the Queensland Aboriginal Act. Did you know anything about the Aboriginal Act?"

Gladys lowered her head but kept her eyes on mine.

"Oh, yes," she replied with a trace of bitterness. "I knew all about the Act, all right. It was still on when I was working." Gladys shifted uneasily in her chair.

"Queensland," she said, resentfully. "It's the only State different from all the rest." She was becoming angry so I thought it prudent to change the subject. "Did you work on stations other than Carandotta?" I asked her.

"I worked on Headingly station."

"Doing the same sort of work?"

"Yes," she nodded. "Doing the same kind of work. That's all they looked for."

"What did you have to do as a housemaid?"

"Oh, make beds, wash up, do the washing, look after kids. Dad used to work there while I was there." She paused for a while. "They used to eat on the wood-heap. I used to eat in the kitchen but all the old cowboys — they used to call them cowboys — they ate on the woodheap. No matter if it rained. They still ate there."

"Gladys, in those days, do you remember if there were many tribes? You know, people getting around in tribes?" She gently bit her bottom lip as she threw her memory back to her childhood.

"Only the Lake Nash mob," she said, finally.[8] "They were still there."

"Did you ever work at Lake Nash?"

"No, we just went for weekends, sort of thing. We would dance. We would just go for the trip and see the mob over there."

"How did you travel to Lake Nash? It would be too far to walk, wouldn't it?"

"Dad had one of those old Holdens," she explained. "I remember every Christmas time we used to go to the Georgina River and have a big corroboree there. Nobody used to have Christmas in town here. Everybody used to do their Christmas shopping here and then go off to the river." Her eyes sparkled and she looked at the ceiling. She smiled slowly as she reminisced. "We used to have an old truck to get around in those days, too," she continued. "We used to get around in that in those days."

"Do they still do it?" I asked.

"Not now," Gladys replied. "One time we used to go. It used to be good. We would go from here and all the town mob would be there and make up their camp. All the station mobs would come then."

"There must have been a lot of people there," I remarked.

"Yes, a big mob. There would be the the Roxborough Downs mob and the Carandotta mob.[9] We used to have big corroborees." The smile faded from her face. "Most of those people have died now," she said, sadly.

"Was there any grog at those Christmas parties?"

"Not as bad as today," she replied. "People didn't drink a lot of beer in those days. These people are sort of overdoing it now though, aren't they?"

I didn't respond to her remark.

Looking across the road from where Harry and Gladys lived I noticed some railway sheds. I remembered that Harry worked for the railways.

"Did the train come through here in those days?" I enquired.

"Yes," Gladys nodded her head. "The train used to come through here. It used to come on Wednesdays. It was an old coal train. They've only just put the other train [diesel] on lately. We used to see the smoke coming from way over the hills there." She waved her arm towards the distant Jimbarella hills.

"I suppose they took a lot of cattle away by train in those days, did they?"

"Oh, yes," she replied, raising her eyebrows. "This was the main train here. The cattle used to come for miles to the train here. This was the main trucking place. They used to walk them in."

"What the heck did you do here for entertainment in those days?" I asked. "I mean, there was no television or radio here, was there?"

"Yes," she corrected, "there was the wireless. We used to listen to the wireless at night. We listened to the hillbillies [country and western music] and 'Dad and Dave'. That's the only thing we had. Perhaps someone would have a gramophone."

"The old wind-up type?"

"Yes. My sister, Dulcie, had one. She was the oldest in the family."

"How many were in your family, Gladys?"

"There were the three of us." She looked at me quickly. "But there were four after. There was seven of us altogether."

"Could they all read and write?"

"Yes. We all went to school. We lost one of our family, though. One passed away."

"What happened?"

"Well, there was this white bloke. He was a Pommie. I think he was the one that did something to her. There was a big court case at Mt Isa. He only went to jail for six months and he came out a free man." She shook her head slowly.

"How many children did you have, Gladys?"

"I only had the one," she replied, shrugging her shoulders. "She's up in Mt Isa now."

"You have brought up a lot of kids though, haven't you? Other people's kids."

"Yes," she said. "Some of the kids lost their mothers. Well, you can't see them without a home, can you?"

"No," I agreed. "How many have you reared?" She bowed her head for a moment, counting with her thumb and her fingers. She took a deep sigh before answering.

"About eight," she concluded. "The Welfare mob came down and seen us. We took them when they were small. They are all married up now. They've got kids of their own."

As we spoke, an old chestnut horse wandered into the yard. Gladys went almost hysterical.

"That 'orse!" she said angrily. "It will eat anything. We left our bread out and it ate the lot. You know, I've even seen it eating meat! It's the first 'orse I've ever seen that will eat meat. Who ever heard of a stupid 'orse eating meat!" She ran down the steps and chased the offending animal out of the yard and up the road. She returned and settled herself into her seat once more, puffing heavily.

"Where did you meet Harry, Gladys?" I asked, after she had caught her breath. Her eyes smiled and twinkled as she looked at me.

"Here," she said, simply.

"How old were you?"

"About eighteen."

I cast my eyes around the room, admiring the decor. My eyes were held by a huge tapestry which hung on the wall. The ornamental design depicted several rearing horses.

"That tapestry looks very effective," I remarked. She followed my gaze and then looked at me.

"My kids gave me that," she said, proudly. "They bought it for me as a Mother's Day present. They bought it for me when they were going to school."

"You've got about all you want," I said with admiration. "Television, video recorder, washing machine. I also like your new car. There is no doubt about it, Harry has worked very hard. He deserves it."

Gladys looked at me sheepishly. "You know what happened?" she said. "When we had the old ute, Harry was riding in the back of it in Mt Isa one night. The police pulled us up and told Harry that he was not allowed to ride in the back. Yet I've seen the biggest load of white people riding in the back of utility trucks. We were the unlucky poor buggers that got caught." Gladys scowled at the memory. "Anyway, we got booked and it cost us a fine. That's why we bought the new car. We had to have room for the kids."

I remarked on the quality of the water in Dajarra. Gladys screwed up her face.

"You can't lather soap in it," she complained. "When you have a bath you have to use shampoo." She pointed out of the window to a large black tank on the railway property.

"That's good water in those tanks," she said. "But that's for the cattle. The animals get the real good water and we've got to use this hard old bore stuff." She shook her head in disgust. "But they're supposed to be getting good water for us here. I don't know when," she added with a sardonic grin. "They haven't made a bore yet. I suppose they're looking for a good spot."

"One thing is for sure," I remarked. "You don't need much tea in the pot when you use this water." Gladys screwed up her face again. "Ruby's got good water. She carts it to her place in a bucket from those black tanks. When you make tea with this water it goes white-looking. And that taste!"

"I know what you mean," I concurred. "You're better off making strong coffee," Gladys said, as she rose from her chair. "Would you like a cup? I'm going to have one." I assured her that a cup of coffee would be very well received.

"There used to be a well near the creek," she said as she filled the electric jug with "good" water which Harry had brought home from the railway tank. "It was real good water. Just like rain water. But the well went dry."

The jug boiled quickly and soon we were enjoying our coffee.

We were about to continue our conversation when an old Aborigine limped into the yard. He walked with a slight crouch but, even so, he was a tall man. His well-worn corduroy trousers and his orange-striped shirt seemed to hang from his frame. His face was unshaven and flecked with grey. Deep lines furrowed each side of his huge nose and his eyes seemed tired and slightly bloodshot. A "cowboy" style hat capped his bristling white hair. He carried a swag wrapped in green canvas.

"Hullo, Uncle George," Gladys greeted him. "Home for a rest?"

"Ah, yes," he said as he placed his swag on the ground. "Just for the weekend."

The old man sat down wearily onto a wire bedstead which was against the wall in the shade of the house. His name was George Nemo, the cousin-brother whom Jimmy Larkin had mentioned in our conversation at Boulia yesterday.

I struck up a conversation with him and he told me that he had been working at Stockport station for many years. In his early days he had been a stockman on the station. Now, all he does is feed the chickens, do a bit of gardening and attend to various odd jobs around the homestead. On his wrist was a watch with one of the most decorative bands I have ever seen. It was of multi-coloured plaited leather. I nodded towards it.

"That's a nice watchband you have there," I remarked. He fiddled with it for a moment before replying.

"Yes. I plaited it myself. It's only boot laces split up the middle and dyed."

"You've made a very nice job of it," I commented. "What else do you plait?" He slid his bottom lip over the top one and held his head to one side.

"Aw, whips, belts. Bits and things," he said, modestly. I recalled his gait. He had walked with a limp.

"Got a sore foot?" I enquired. He gazed down and rubbed his shin for a few moments before replying.

"Nah," he said, "broke a leg once." So saying, he pulled his trouser leg up above his knee. A huge bulge presented itself. It went entirely around the leg and, on the inside, a jagged outline of broken bone could be seen. He stopped rubbing it before he spoke.

"Bloody thing aches like hell sometimes," he continued. "They reckon it's got something to do with the weather."

On further questioning he told me that a horse had fallen and rolled on him one day while he was out mustering cattle. He was a very vague man and I found it difficult to hold a running conversation with him.

He pulled the leg of his trousers back down, rose from the stretcher and wandered off down the dusty road towards the pub.

"Be back in a minute," he called to me over his shoulder. He soon returned with a carton of beer tucked under his thin, bony arm. I realised that any conversation with him in the immediate future would be hopeless. The old bloke had finished his allotted tasks on the station and now it was time for a binge. Well, why not?

I informed Gladys that I would be back later and wandered off to see if Ruby was feeling any better. She was asleep. I spent a few minutes speaking with an Aborigine who had recently returned from Urandangie and told him of my plans to visit the area. He advised me that the older members of the Warluwa tribe which somtimes frequents Urandangie were making ready for a trip to the head of the Georgina River. As these were the people with whom I proposed to work, my visit to Urandangie brooked no delay. I would leave very early on Monday. I hoped Ruby would be over her illness by then. If not, then I would have to proceed without her. If this happened, she would be most disappointed.

"A lot were lying around . . . shot"

Fortunately, when Monday arrived, Ruby was on her feet and rearing to go. We packed sufficient food and water and set out as the horizon began to show the pink tinge of dawn. After we turned off the main highway towards Urandangie, the road was unbelievable. Sharp gravel, enormous potholes, bulldust; it was all there.

Now, here in Queensland, we have a Minister for the Main Roads. He claims that the roads in Queensland are in tiptop shape. Well, I would like to drag him over every single kilometre of the road between that turn-off and Urandangie!

We arrived in Urandangie in a cloud of fine, white dust. The wind was almost at gale force. Unfortunately we were too late as most of the tribe had already left for the Georgina and they were not expected to return until late in the week. So, the first thing Ruby and I did was to light a fire in order to make a brew of tea and grill some sausages we'd brought with us. The only suitable place we could find that would give us some protection from the wind was in the dry bed of the once mighty Georgina River. I recalled Ruby's jibe about having to hide behind a tree to bait your hook and I was tempted to ask Ruby if she thought we should run away from the fish but, as she was getting cranky with the wind for blowing her fire out, I decided not to stir her.

After washing the dust from our throats and gnawing on some rather overcooked snags, I decided to have a look around to see if there was anyone with whom I could have a yarn. It did not take long for, sitting under a stunted tree on the side of the road, was a very old Aborigine. One eye was closed and the other was under attack by a myriad of small bush flies. He was dressed in a faded grey and very ragged dustcoat half-tucked into a pair of ill-fitting trousers. He wore no shirt and this emphasised the protruding bones of his frame; he was thin almost to the point of emaciation. On his feet was an old pair of black shoes with no laces. His face was covered by a long grey straggly beard through which a snub, bulbous nose protruded. His long, slender fingers ended with curled, overgrown fingernails. He looked pathetic, sitting there alone.

I introduced myself and was extremely surprised to find that he spoke particularly good English. As I shook his hand, his face opened in a toothless grin. He was known as Cyclone Jack. I started yarning to him and gave him a fair idea about what I was after.

"What are you doing here?" I asked him. "Why didn't you go to the Georgina with the others?"

"Ah, too old for that caper now," he replied, shifting from one bony buttock onto the other. "I can't travel those long distances any more. I would only hold the others back and be a bloody nuisance. They wouldn't take me anyway, even if I wanted to."

"Why the bloody hell are you sitting there in the wind and the dust?"

"I was hoping to get away from these bastards of

flies," he explained logically. "Sometimes the wind blows them away but it's not working this time, eh?" He waved furiously at the flies as he spoke. "What would you like to know?" His soft voice conveyed to me that he was reasonably well-educated. I remarked upon this and he shrugged his shoulders.

"Where were you educated?" I asked.

"Well, it was in a little place called Loganholme. It's not far from Beenleigh. You know Beenleigh?"

"Yes," I answered. "I have been through there. It's down past Brisbane."

"Yair, that's right," he smiled. "That's the place. There was a small school there one time. But I didn't go to it."

Jack noticed my puzzled look. "It was a one man set-up, you know," he continued. "The teacher lived close to where we camped and I got to know him pretty well. I just couldn't say why but he somehow took a liking to me and he gave me this schooling. He gave me a lot of schooling in his spare time. Mainly in the afternoons and the weekends. I used to chop the chips for his missus, you know." He looked at me for my reaction. I nodded in understanding, thinking that this must have been not long before World War I.

"You must have been a good learner," I remarked.

"As a matter of fact, I enjoyed that schooling, you know. I used to like doing those things with the slate and pencil. It took a bit of time for me to learn to read but once I got the hang of it I couldn't seem to get enough to read. Only kid stuff, you know. But I got better later on." He laughed lightly as he spoke of his school days. "'Course, there wasn't much stuff to read in them days. It's different now." He looked away from me and a frown covered his face.

"You know," he said, turning back to me, "I went

through there about four years ago and I couldn't recognise it. There are shops and houses there now. I think even the old school has been pulled down." He smiled as some past event sprang into his mind.

"By gee, I used to have a lot of fun around there." His eyes brightened as he recalled the happiness he had enjoyed in those younger days. He swung furiously at the flies which seemed to be increasing in number.

"Hang on a minute," I said to him. I walked over to my vehicle and returned with a can of insect repellent and handed it to Jack. He took it and, turning into the wind, closed his eyes and sprayed the mist over his face and head. He then gave his arms a similar drowning before handing the can back to me. I gave myself a good dousing also.

"Bloody good stuff, that," Jack remarked. "Better than that citronella shit we used during the war. Look, they've gone already."

"You remember the war, then?" I asked. "Where were you during the war?"

He looked vacantly at the sky for a few moments.

"Ah, yes," he remembered. "I was camped at a place called Beaudesert. I used to cut timber there. I worked for a mob called Hancock and Gore."

"When you were a boy, what did you do? I mean, how did you pass the time?"

"Yard building," he answered. "I used to build cattle yards."

"Whereabouts?"

"Lake Nash. A place called Lake Nash. It's a cattle station, you know."

"What age were you when you did that work, Jack?" I asked. The question puzzled him for a while as he struggled with his memory.

"Aw, buggered if I know, Bill," he said, shaking his head slowly. "When I was a little one."

As he spoke he seemed preoccupied in sending little puffs of white dust up into the air with his toe and watching the wind carry it away. The action amused him and he smiled.

"Jack," I interrupted his little game, "do you still do the corroboree?" He let out a hissing sound as he pulled those lips into his toothless mouth again.

"Aw, noooo," he answered. "I'm too old for that now. But we still got it. We still have them on Ardmore station. I still sing corroboree songs sometimes though."

"Could you sing a corroboree song now?"

"Yes," he answered without hesitation. Without further ado he threw back his scraggy head and broke out into a screechy song. I tried desperately not to laugh but, just as my lungs were about to burst, I let out with a full-bellied roar.

"Aw, shit." Jack looked at me in astonishment. "Don't you like it?" I sensed that, inwardly, he was laughing too. He was a great old fellow and I knew I hadn't hurt his feelings by laughing. He seemed pleased that he was able to amuse me in such measure.

"Well, actually, Jack," I replied to his question. "I reckon if you were singing with your mob they would chase you into the bush." We both laughed.

"Yes, I know," Jack replied. "I was only joking with you."

He really was a playful old bloke and full of fun. He braced his thin shoulders as squarely as he could and took several deep breaths and wheezed out.

"I'll sing proper for you now," he said. He took a final deep breath and began to sing. In spite of the dust and the flies, Jack's mouth opened and closed in unison with his clapping hands.

First a low note, up to a higher pitch, completely oblivious to anything or anybody around. His register rose even higher.

"Nyar, Nyar, Nyar," he sang, his yellowed eyeballs rolling in my direction.

When the song ended, he blinked his wrinkled eyelids and licked the dust from his lips.

"That's about the initiation ceremony," he explained.

"Sounds good." I patted him lightly on the shoulder. "Very impressive," I assured him. I took advantage of his mention of initiation. "Tell me, Jack, where is the boy who is to be made into a man during the initiation corroboree?"

"Oh, they hide him away somewhere," he replied.

"Would he be on his own?"

"No. There might be three or four of them."

"Jack, supposing those boys didn't want to have their foreskins cut; could they refuse or run away?" Old Cyclone Jack compressed his lips and slowly shook his head. His eyes didn't leave mine.

"Oh," he said, "they can't run away. The people would grab them. No, they can't run away."

"What happens after they have had their foreskins cut? What do the tribe do to them?"

"Oh, well," he replied, casually, "they put them in the bush, you see. They've got to stay away from everybody. Even their mother. They've got to stay away for two or three weeks. Then they're allowed back. They're not on their own, you know."

"Not on their own?" I questioned.

"No. They've got people with them to look after them. You know, to get them tucker and that." The old man pulled gently at the lobe of his ear for a moment. "But, you know," he continued, "things are a lot different now, eh. You know, mothers can see their sons and all that. All this tribal thing . . . it's all lost now."

"You mean, your customs and your culture are lost?" He wrinkled up his face and looked at me quizzically.

"Well, yes," he replied. "Oh, they still do a lot of these things out west but it's nothing like way back."

The wind had reached almost gale force now and it was becoming impossible to record. Jack's words were whisked away on the wind and the dust blew up in gritty clouds. My tape recorder ceased to function and literally ground to a halt. Jack was covered with a layer of white dust and his beard stood out at a ridiculous angle. He cautiously eased himself up with a shaky arm, mumbling about the dust. He got to his feet and, gathering his worn-out dustcoat around him, moved off towards a small rusty galvanised iron shed, motioning me to follow. Inside the shed, in one corner, was a "doss-down" bed consisting of old mattress fibre and leaves. A makeshift table fashioned from pine boxes was in another. Several more boxes which served as seats completed the furnishings. In the centre of the room was a small fire made between some large boulders. Jack busied himself by placing some kindling onto the fire and, presently, small tongues of flame rose lazily into the air.

"I'll put the billy on," he said, as he balanced a blackened old billy can upon the rocks. "You feel like a cup?"

"My oath," I assured him. "It's good to get out of that wind, too." Jack took two chipped and battered enamel mugs from the table and rinsed them in a plastic bucket of not-too-clean water and replaced them upon the table. He waved me to one of the pine box seats and I gingerly sat down.

"Is there anything I can do?" I asked dutifully.

"Ah, no. I can manage this," he said, as he scratched some coals around the billy can.

It was not long before the water began to bubble and Jack tossed a rather large handful of tea into it. He filled the two mugs and pushed one over to me. I really don't think I have ever swallowed tea like that before. It caught the inside of the throat and hung on, causing an involuntary grimace.

"Christ! You like your tea strong, don't you, Jack," I remarked.

"Aw, well," he replied, squeakily. "It keeps the kidneys working and, besides, you don't need to drink so much of it."

"You're not wrong," I answered, between gritted teeth. "What brand of tea is it? I don't think I've tasted it before."

"Oh, it's not tea," Jack exclaimed.

I felt my countenance change rapidly as I looked quickly at the black billy can and then at the brown paper bag which contained the "tea". My eyes rolled skyward.

"Christ! What have I done?" I asked, suspiciously. "What is it?"

"It's dried bottlebrush leaves," he replied simply.

"Ahhhh," I spat. "It tastes bloody awful! Struth! How the hell can you drink the stuff?" For reply, Jack muttered something under his breath and then began to laugh lightly.

"I thought you'd like a bit of bush stuff. We drink it all the time."

"Well," I relented. "I don't suppose it's too bad. I've

tasted worse things, that's for sure. But, right now, I can't think of anything."

Old Cyclone Jack almost doubled up with his croaky laugh. He took my mug and tossed its contents out the door. He moved over to the table and opened a bottle of pre-used and re-dried coffee grains and brewed a mug of coffee.

"I got the coffee from a bloke that was here, one time," he said, as he handed me the mug. "I've used it a couple of times but it's still got life in it yet." I smiled and thanked him. The coffee, although it was watery, brought back my sense of humour once more.

"It's a pity you couldn't go to the Georgina with your tribe," I remarked. Jack frowned a little as he tossed the remainder of the vile liquid down his throat.

"Oh, that's not my tribe, you know," he said, looking at me quickly. "My tribe no more."

"What do you mean, 'no more'?"

"Well," he explained. "Although I'm here at Urandangie, this is not my country. My country is 'way down south'."

"Where would that be, Jack?"

"Down near Beenleigh. I come from around the Logan River."

"That's south of Brisbane, isn't it?"

"Aw, yes. It's a big area down there. It is part of what is known as the Bandjalang group."

"Do you know your Dreaming?"

"No, I don't remember," Jack confessed. "I've forgotten that years ago. I suppose I should know, but I don't."

"Fair enough," I said. "You're not the only one. There are many Aborigines who don't remember their Dreaming."

"Yes, I know. It's a shame, that." Cyclone Jack

stood up and gave himself a shake. White dust floated from him as he ran his hand through his thin, grey hair.

"Jack, if you come from Beenleigh country, why are you living right up here?"

"Oh, I been here for a long time," he said as he resumed his seat. "When my old father died, I worked my way up this way and I stayed."

"Have you been here ever since?"

"Just about. Except when the war was on. I went cutting timber down at Beaudesert then."

"Why did you come back to this dry and dusty place? You would have been better off down there, wouldn't you?"

"I don't like that place down there," he answered. "All my family don't like that place either." He rubbed his hand across his face and looked sideways at me. "Bad things happen there once, you know. Very bad."

"What do you mean, Jack?" I asked, as casually as I could. "What happened to you down there?"

"Not to me," he said, quickly. "To my tribe. They get all killed. My father tell me about it. He learned it from his father . . . my grandfather, you know." He seemed to be getting agitated. The information he had just given to me pricked my ears. I could smell something and I got the feeling that this old man wanted to share with me his knowledge of what had happened so long ago.

"I would like to hear about it, Jack," I coaxed him.

"Oh, I'll tell you," he replied. "I'll tell you all right. The trouble is, it is a long story. You might not have time to listen."

"How about twelve months, Jack?" I replied flippantly. Perhaps my manner seemed impudent but it wasn't meant to be. I simply wanted to assure him that I had plenty of time at my disposal. Suddenly I felt an urgent desire to scratch. I looked down and at least two million ground fleas were attacking my legs. I stood up quickly, knocking the flimsy box seat over, and began a counter attack. "Bloody hell," I expostulated, brushing vigorously at my legs.

"That's them ground fleas," explained Jack. "Bloody plenty here. All over. I rub kerosene on, that stops them. There's some in a tin in the corner, there." I rubbed the kerosense-soaked rag over my legs. Instant relief.

Cyclone Jack nodded as he drew out a crumpled packet of tobacco.

"Here," I offered. "Would you like one of these?"

I tossed a packet of Hallmark Filters across the table. He took one out and lit it with a coal from the fire. After blowing clouds of blue smoke into the air he shifted on his box and faced me squarely. His eyes darted from my face to the floor and back to me again. He seemed to be in a very agitated state. I sat watching him, never dreaming that the story Cyclone Jack was about to unfold would be the most horrifying and astounding story I had ever heard.

"Well," he began. "It was in 1859 or 1860, I'm not sure. In those days the settlers and the squatters were in top gear. They came . . ."

"Hang on," I interrupted. "What do you mean by 'top gear'?"

"Well, they were busy growing their cattle and building up their herds," he explained. "They were after as much grazing land as they could get. A lot of them — not all of them, you know — chased the blackfellas, whole tribes of them, away from the land that the white fellas needed. Those tribes they couldn't chase off, well, they were either shot or poisoned off — or both. Some tribes were killed right out."

"Poisoned? How were the blacks poisoned?" I asked.

"Oh, well," Jack answered grimly, "the white men would leave flour around for them blackfellas. But, that flour was full of arsenic. Them blackfellas found this out too late." He shook his head slowly.

"Yes," I replied. "I've read about such things. I believe that the settlers' guns ran a bit hot, too, from shooting blacks."

"That's true," Jack nodded his head vigorously.

"Although a lot of squatters shot thousands of blackfellas, the Aboriginal police — police on horses, you know. They called them the Native Mounted Police. They killed thousands too."

"Mounted Police," I pretended. "What was the Mounted Police?"

The muscles of his jaw knotted as he took out another cigarette from the packet which lay opened upon the table. He lit it from his butt and puffed furiously for a few moments.

"They were those black trackin' bastards that used to go around with them white police and shoot other blackfellas," he replied, smoke billowing from his mouth as he spoke. He sprang from his seat and came towards me, obviously in an extreme state of anxiety. I was thankful that he was not a Kalkadoon![10]

"It was those mongrels that killed off my tribe," he continued as he stood shaking before me.

"Shit, Jack," I defended. "I only asked. I don't know anything about native bloody coppers." He relaxed and returned to his seat, the energy now spent from his skinny frame.

"Aw, yes," he said, as he sat and faced me once more. "There were hundreds of them."

"But why?" I asked. "Why would those blackfellows

want to shoot other blackfellows? Wouldn't they all be mates?" Cyclone Jack's eyes widened.

"No bloody fear," he answered, his nostrils flared. "They came from another tribe, see. The tribe they came from would be enemies of the Bandjalang mob, and most of the other mobs. Those troopers were brought up by the white police officers. They brought them up from as far as four hundred miles sometimes." He sat silently for a while, puffing urgently on his cigarette. I waited for him to continue his narrative.

"You know," he said at last, "most white people think that, just because the blackfella has got black skin, that they are all bloody mates. No bloody fear! They all got their enemies just like the white people. Look at all them white fella that fight; look at all them white fella what kill each other in them wars."

Old Jack was becoming quite excited and I noticed that he was discarding his more educated manner of speaking.

"Don't forget, it was them friggin' blackfellas that were brought up here what got rid of my tribe!"

"How can you be so sure of that?" I challenged, deciding to disregard his change in temperament. "If all this happened back in 1860, over 120 years ago, surely a lot of what you are telling me could be hear-say. It's a long time ago." I was really pressing old Jack to see if he would falter. He turned and faced me squarely, his shoulders stiffening.

"It's not bloody hearsay, Bill," he said, vehemently. "It's not hearsay at all. My father, him tell me the story when I was a boy. His father was belong to that mob."

"What tribe was that?"

"Not sure," he answered. "I told you before, they

were all part of Bandjalang. That tribe covered a lot of territory." A fire dwelled in his black eyes as he sat looking at me.

"I would be very interested in what your father told you," I urged. "Would it be against your laws or customs if you were to tell me?"

"No, it wouldn't," he replied, his face softening a little. "If you've got the time to listen, I'll tell you about it. I'd like to tell you."

"Well," I reassured him. "I certainly have the time." He fiddled with the buttonhole of his dustcoat.

"Aw, right then," he said. "This is the story my father told me — just as his father told him." Old Jack settled back, lit up another smoke and leaned back against the wall.

"It was just before Christmas," he began. "It was 1860, I think. My grandfather and some of his tribe were out hunting early one morning — you know, when the wallabies come out to feed. They were walking along the flat near the creek. There were about five of them. His uncle was one. I have tried to trace their movements — this was years ago, you know — and the nearest I could work out was Christmas Creek. Anyway, they were about to cross the creek when one of the mob looked up and saw some of these police riding towards them." He lolled his head to one side, no doubt visualising the scene of the native police on horseback.

"In those days, those police were bad news," he continued, flicking his eyes from me to the floor. "They were a mob of blackfellas from other tribes that lived a long way away, like I said before. My grandfather and his friends tried to run away because they knew what to expect. These police had guns and they knew how to use them. They were taught by the white Pom officers. The first to go down was his uncle. The rest of the mob ran for their lives but they were not quick enough for the guns. My grandfather was one that lived to tell the tale." Cyclone Jack was so absorbed in telling me his story that he had forgotten about the cigarette he held between his fingers. As it burned down to his fingers he let out a high-pitched squeak and waved his hand furiously.

"Eeeee. Bastard!" he squealed. However unsympathetic it may have appeared, I screamed with laughter. I reckon, for a few moments, old Jack became as nimble as a two-year-old! He jumped up from his seat and danced around on his toes, flinging his hand around as if he had been bitten by a black snake. But what really convulsed me was the fact that, as Jack suddenly jumped up, he let go with a fart. The poor old bugger was too concerned about his singed fingers to be embarrassed. He plunged the hand into the bucket of water which was used to make the "tea". I made a mental note and, wiping the streams from my eyes, brought his attention back to our conversation.

"What happened then?" I asked, offering him another smoke. He glared at me accusingly but took the cigarette nevertheless.

"Where was I?" he asked, lighting the smoke.

"You were telling me how your grandfather got away from those native police," I reminded him.

"Oh, yes, that's right. Well, my grandfather made a wide circle back to where the tribe had its camp. When he got close he knew something was wrong because he heard a lot of noise. The camp was being hit by more of those mounted police. A lot were lying around because they were shot."

I winced as I visualised what the scene must have been like. As Jack's story soaked in, I had a vague recollection of having read something, somewhere, about such an attack.

"It must have been a hell of a shock for your grandfather to see the camp like that," I remarked.

Toothless, he sucked his lips in again in that now characteristic fashion, making a grotesque face.

"When my grandfather get to camp, those police saw him and shot at him, but they missed. He noticed his boy being run over by a horse so he ran over and picked him up and ran into a patch of bush."

The boy was Jack's father and the bush he referred to was the Dugandan scrubs, a heavily wooded area near Fassifern.

Jack looked thoughtfully at the ground before continuing. "Many years ago," he said, "I tried to find out about the story my father told me. I found out something but I didn't understand it. It was about an attack on that Dugandan place by the blacktrackers. There must have been a lot of bush there but it's no more now. All gone." His face wrinkled in thought.

"That's where my grandfather's tribe stayed; what was left of them, that is." He turned his head up toward the ceiling, obviously trying desperately to recall long-lost memories.

"Now that I think of it," he said, quietly, "my grandfather's tribe was called Telemon. They used to often stay around Telemon Station. That's why they were called them, I think." [11]

"Can you remember what that information was, or where you found it?" He looked at the roof again, eyes tightly shut.

"Aw, bugger if I know, Bill," he admitted, after a while. "No, I can't remember that one." He shook his head slowly. "It was a long time ago, but it was in a government book that I read it."

"Don't worry about it," I consoled him. "I'll have a good look around when I get back to Brisbane." He nodded in agreement but once more began flicking his eyes around in obvious agitation.

"What I tell you is true, Bill," he assured me. "When they shot my uncle in the thigh — my father's uncle — they went up to him and shot him in the head. The mongrels were laughing all this time. It was pretty bloody crook what them buggers done." He was plainly very angry and his fibrous beard was thrust out in a pugnacious manner. He lit up another smoke and twirled it thoughtfully in his fingers.

"Anyway," he continued. "They all got killed except my grandfather. When the shooting started, they jumped into the water. I think it must be Christmas Creek. But my grandfather took off for the bush on his own. He reckon he could see the water go red when they were hit. They had never . . ."

"Hang on a minute," I interrupted. "When your grandfather ran into the bush, didn't the police chase him?"

"I don't know," he admitted. "They wouldn't have caught him though. It was his territory and he knew it good."

"I suppose so," I replied. "What happened then?"

"When my grandfather got close to the camp he said he could smell some funny smell. When he looked he saw all these people had been put on a fire. That was where the smell was coming from."

We both sat silently, absorbed in our own thoughts. No doubt, Jack was thinking of his father's words. As for myself, I conjured up vivid mental images of what the camp must have been like. Weeks later, I was to discover just what such a scene was like:

> The first surmise was that it was some early kangaroo hunter,

but the crack was too sharp for that, and the number of discharges too numerous to allow of such a supposition bearing a second thought, and a rush in the direction of the camp was immediately made by those who were so early a-foot, where a scene presented itself alike brutal on the part of the perpetrators, and revolting to the feelings of those who saw it.

The native camp was deserted, but around the fires nearest to the township lay scanty garments of men, gins, and piccaninnees, many of them saturated with blood, while the tracks of the fugitives could easily be traced by the trail of blood leading from the fires in every direction. At the fire nearest the creek, which separates the camp from the township, and around which a number of blacks had apparently been sleeping, two pools of blood and brains showed where foul murder had been perpetrated, and a gin's clothing, all stained with blood, was also found, exactly as if the unfortunate black had just left the articles on finding herself wounded. A little further on, closer to the fire, where one person, probably an old man, had passed the night, another puddle of blood and brains was found, and the surrounding ground bore all the traces of the flight of wounded men, and of dead bleeding bodies having been dragged over it. The first body discovered was that of a black boy called Tommy, and better known as "Mr Patterson", from having been a stock-driver in the employment of Mr Joseph Patterson, which led him to jocularly adopt the name, and stamped him as a well-known character in the district. The poor fellow was found lying in a water hole with three wounds, one through the arm, another through the chest, and a third through the brain.

The next corpse found was a little lubra, stiff and stark, concealed under a bush, but up to the present time no trace of any other dead bodies has been found; several of the wounded, however, have made their appearance, amongst whom is a girl with a bullet through her thigh, a little boy also wounded in the leg, and a poor old lame man who could scarcely hobble along, from the effects of disease. The body of the old man has since been found dead, on one of the heights in the neighbourhood of the town, amonst the scrub, where he had either been shot down or had attempted to conceal himself.

Scattered over the bush, were to be seen several black troopers, belonging to the Native Police, in close pursuit of the fugitives, and who, by the way of recreation, amused themselves by shooting with their revolvers at the dogs which were either running master-less or following the general stampede. It was only too evident that a fearful slaughter had been committed, and a *report* gave as its cause, that on the previous day a shepherd's hut, on one Mr Archer's stations, had been entered by the blacks, the shepherd murdered, mutilated, and disembowelled, and the hut robbed of the rations it contained. One of the troopers is said to have told this tale to more than one person, and to have added that their instructions were to "spare none". Be this as it may, *there was not a word of truth in it,* with the exception, that two stray blacks of a *different tribe* had entered a shepherd's hut and stolen some sugar and tea, but had *used no violence, nor committed any outrage*.

The facts, as I have been able to ascertain them, simply are that a robbery of rations from a shepherd's hut having been committed, the Native Police were called upon to follow and capture the thieves, and with the services of a black tracker, they supposed that they had been able to find them in the neighbourhood of Morinish. Camping out for the night, the troopers and their commandant must have started before daylight, and caught all the unsuspicious natives asleep at their camp, and the horrible tragedy and disgraceful butchery I have described, followed before the sun had risen, which has been palliated by calling it a warning to the blacks not to rob shepherds' huts in future.[12]

Had my countenance betrayed me?

I camped at Urandangie that night. I found a reasonable spot behind a huge coolibah tree on the bank of the Georgina River. Ruby had some friends who were camped a little way along the track near an old windmill so she was all right for the night. The wind died down somewhat but it was still necessary to tuck oneself snugly into a sleeping bag. I rose early and was absolutely astonished at the number of kangaroos grazing on the opposite side of the river bed. Without exaggeration, there would have been in excess of a hundred roos, backs arched and their front "hands" scratching at the roots of the stunted Mitchell grass. I gave the bonnet of the Datsun a resounding thump and the roos slowly raised their heads, looked at me for a moment and then resumed their feeding, not being the slightest bit alarmed at my presence. I wandered down to the small shop where I was able to scrounge some water for a bit of a wash. My hair was full of dust which made it impossible to control — a passerby could not be blamed for mistaking me for a wild man from Borneo.

I wondered how old Cyclone Jack was coping. I looked across towards his little rusty shack and, sure enough, small wisps of smoke were issuing from beneath the tin roof. He strolled outside and, on seeing me, beckoned me over. When I arrived he smiled a gummy smile and asked me how I got on for the night. I told him where I spent the night and he looked cross.

"Ah, heck," he said. "You could have dossed down in here."

"That would have been a good idea," I lied, mentally feeling my body covered with ground fleas. "Why is it that we think of these things too late?"

"Ready for some more stories?" he asked.

"Sure," I replied. "But it's a bit bloody early to be magging, isn't it?" Jack licked his lips and peered at the early morning sun. He did not reply to my question. Instead, he walked back inside his hut and fiddled around with the fire and soon bright flames replaced the lazy wisps of smoke. He filled the big old billy can and balanced it on one of the rocks. I was pleased to note that he had refilled the bucket with sparkling clean water. I walked inside and took up my usual position on the pine box. Jack came across and sat on the other.

"You know," he said, wasting no time in getting back to yesterday's subject. "My grandfather pissed off from that place."

"What place?" I asked, trying to recall the place he had mentioned.

"Where he went into that bushy Dugandan scrub to hide," Jack replied. "He went looking for the rest of his tribe."

"Some of them got away, did they? I thought they had all been stonkered by those police."

"Oh, no," he replied. "Some of the tribe got away all right. But they just scattered. Some went down towards the coast and some went down to Mt Lindsay. You know where that is?"

"Yes, I know," I answered. "But do you know why those black troopers attacked your grandfather's camp?"

"Oh, well, I couldn't really say. They were blamed for robbing a hut, I think. I think I read it in that book I was telling you about." He shook his head and spat on the ground with disgust. "But those bloody bastards often got stuck into a lot of people just for fun. True. They used to do that sometimes."

I later discovered the reason for the attack. A hut had been robbed of some tobacco and blankets. The hut was on a property owned by John Hardie, a settler who, on discovering the robbery, sent a letter of complaint to the Native Police Headquarters at Sandgate. The investigation of the complaint was detailed to Lieutenant Frederick Wheeler and his detachment. The detachment arrived at Hardie's property on 2 January 1861. Wheeler's reputation was one of cruelty and sadism.

"What happened then? I mean, to the rest of the tribe? You know, the ones that got away from the camp."

"Well," Jack replied, stabbing the air with a roughly rolled cigarette, "my grandfather found one of his friends not far from the camp after those bastards got stuck into them. He was pretty hurt. He told my grandfather where he thought the rest of the tribe had moved off to." He looked away from me and studied the ground in front of him, no doubt waiting for me to ask another question. As I watched in silence, his lips didn't stop moving.

"And where did they end up, Jack?" I probed.

"They walked a long, long way, I believe. They all met up somewhere and they all walked around Mt Lindsay and came up again behind the Dugandan scrub. On the other side there, they ran into another mob. I looked it up on a big map and I think this mob was known as Jukambe mob. These people used to live around Telemon Station, I think.

"Anyway," Jack continued, "they got on with them so they stayed together. One of the tribe had married into my grandfather's tribe 'way back'. So they were friendly, you know."

"How many were in that mob, Jack?"

"I couldn't really say," Jack replied. "But I reckon there would be about two or three hundred. That Telemon mob was a big mob, you know." He rose from his seat and walked towards the smoky fire. He prodded the coals for a moment.

"You want a cup of tea?" he asked. "I'm going to have one."

"Oh, no thanks, Jack," I answered quickly. "I'll stick with the strainings of the coffee."

He poured some boiling water into the mug which contained the second-hand coffee grains and then he tossed a handful of "tea" into the remainder of the water in the billy can.

We sat silently for a while, sipping our respective beverages. Occasionally Jack rubbed his gums together as that disgusting liquid passed over his lips. My coffee was really not much better but at least it disguised the colour of the water!

"Tell me, Jack," I prompted, "what happened after your grandfather joined with the Telemon mob? Did he stay with them for long?"

"Oh, yes," he replied. "But they were still in trouble."

"What do you mean, Jack? What sort of trouble?"

"Oh, well. They were still hunted and chased, you know. They reckon that those Telemon people were no good. They were supposed to be a mob of trouble-makers." He made a fist to emphasise his words. "They reckon they used to spear cattle."

"Did they?"

"I don't know. Probably did, you know. Them white settlers and their squatter mates chased the blackfella's tucker way inland. You know, the emu, kangaroo and all that. What they couldn't chase, they sooled the dogs onto them. Yes, I think they probably speared some cattle." He looked bitter as he knocked the dregs from his mug. "I know they walked a long way, all around the place."

"Because they were hunted?"

"Partly, I think. My grandfather said that the Mounted Police were always after them."

"Where did they walk to? Do you know?"

"Well, my father said they went from Dugandan but before they could get there, buggered if those black bastards caught up with them again."

"What . . ." I began, but Cyclone Jack anticipated my question.

"Well," he said, "the few what were left were crossing a paddock owned by a bloke called Hardie. When they were about halfway across the paddock, who should ride up but this Wheeler bloke with his bunch of murdering black mongrels. They shot three of them but the rest of them ran to the cover of the scrub. My grandfather said that those mongrels scouted around and picked up a heap of wood and tried to burn the three poor bastards that were shot." Jack stopped talking and went limp. It was as if, for him, life had come to a stop for a few seconds.

I understood the emotion which had suddenly overtaken him. Cyclone Jack, whilst probably beyond despair, was quite susceptible to anguish.

Once again, his narrative was to prove fairly accurate as I discovered later. Evidence supplied to the Select Committee on the Native Police Force, 1861, showed that, indeed, three Aborigines had been shot on the property of John Hardie and that an attempt had been made to incinerate them. The attempt failed and the result was, according to Dr Henry Challinor, the District Coroner who inspected the remains, that "the bodies were so highly decomposed, that when we came to examine them and to turn them over, they fell to pieces". When Challinor was asked by the Committee Chairman if he considered that the evidence brought before him was sufficiently conclusive to warrant his assumption that Lieutenant Wheeler was the cause of death in the case of these blacks, Challinor answered, "I do."[13]

"They went down to Mt Lindsay," Jack continued, "but buggered if those black bastards caught up with them there. Wheeler and his mob."

"This Wheeler must have been a keen sort of bloke," I remarked. "He must have wanted your grandfather's tribe badly to ride all that way. It must be over a hundred miles from Sandgate to Mt Lindsay."

"I think he must have hated blacks," Jack observed.

We yarned on for an hour or so. Jack's responses were becoming less frequent. He looked longingly across to his bed. Although it was still early in the morning — it would have been about 9.00 a.m. — I could see that the old man was tired. His eyes were blinking and he dropped his head onto his chest.

"Jack," I said, gently, "you ought to have a bit of a rest. It looks as if you didn't sleep at all last night." He lifted his head and gazed over to me.

"As a matter of fact, Bill," he admitted, "I didn't

sleep much. Bugger if I know, I just lie and think about them old days. My old father. Things. They all seem long away now. I thought I forget those things but, last night, they just keep jumping into my head. I can't sleep! Now, I'm bloody tired."

Although the wail of his voice and the pained expression on his face seemed comical, I could not laugh. Rather, it was somewhat tragic to watch this frail old man, this grimy, unkempt, lovable and neglected little man whose stoop and frailty suggested to me that soon he would return to his Dreaming. It was as if he understood my thoughts for he slowly turned and faced me, his deep eyes squinting and his lips parting in a slight smile. He nodded slowly then looked away. Did he understand? Had my countenance betrayed me?

"Jack," I said, hurriedly, "why don't you have a bit of a camp? I'll pop back later on. Maybe we can talk a bit more then, OK?"

"I think I will do that, Bill," he agreed. He rose from his seat and, picking up an old, grey, worn blanket, he shook it so vigorously that he almost threw himself off his feet. I laughed quietly to myself and patted him gently on the shoulder.

"See you later," I called out as I walked out of the shed. I returned to my vehicle where Ruby was speaking to a group of young people, one of whom was desperately trying to open a tin of camp pie with an old mower blade.

After I'd greeted Ruby, and introductions to her friends had been completed, I took a can opener from under the seat of my Datsun and handed it to the now bad-tempered blackfellow.

"Hang on to it," I told him. "I think I've got another one in my toolbox." He looked up, smiled his thanks and went to work on the tin of camp pie. He sure was one hungry blackfellow!

The time was only ten-thirty. It was too early to go back to visit Cyclone Jack. He would probably still be sleeping. I wandered over to the small shop which services the few homes in Urandangie and stayed yarning to the woman behind the counter for about an hour. When I left the shop I noticed the crowd of young people to whom Ruby had introduced me sitting around the windmill a little way off toward the river. Ruby was nowhere in sight so I crossed over to them. A small fire was spiralling up thin ropes of smoke into the now still, hot air. I wondered idly why they would want a fire in this heat. After I threaded myself through the barbed wire fence which kept the cattle from scratching and rubbing themselves against the windmill, I asked them where Ruby was. A young, lean Aborigine waved his arm carelessly in the direction of the river.

"She gone down dere," he said. "She go look for gwanna. Might be someting else dere." I nodded my understanding. I decided not to go down to the river because it would be just my luck to scare off something that Ruby had lined up. I heard one of the young people say that they were going to see if they could hunt up a "gwanna" somewhere. As I had nothing to do I decided to go with them. I had no boots on, but neither did anybody else. We all strolled off along the top of the river bank. I lagged behind a bit so as not to impede their hunting expertise. They were quite a bit ahead of me when they disappeared from sight over the bank. I walked slowly until I had reached the top of the bank when suddenly a giant goanna came hurtling over the top and headed straight towards me. It was closely followed by the mob of whooping blackfellows, waving enormous sticks in readiness to let fly at the frantic saurian. Luckily they spotted me and held their grip on the waddies. But the goanna came straight ahead, probably hoping that I was a tree. Just as it was about to climb one, I neatly sidestepped. Not neatly enough! The black and yellow monster ran clear between my legs, its wet, slimy tongue dragging across my bare feet. I really don't know how high into the air I jumped but my companions told me I seemed to hang there. They were too overcome with mirth to continue their pursuit. Not me! I had a mental picture of my foot had the brute latched onto me. Two of my new-found friends were rolling around on the grass, clutching their stomachs.

"Fuck you for a joke!" I expostulated. "You're a dangerous mob of bastards." I was deadly serious in my remarks but they were not taken seriously, which only added insult to injury. They laughed even louder. Within a few seconds I, too, saw the hilarity of the past few seconds. I sat down beside them and laughed with them, albeit a somewhat shaky laugh. As we made our way back to the windmill, a cloud of dust was seen coming along the road. As it got closer we could see that it was a police paddy wagon. The young Aborigine who had spoken to me earlier appeared to be nervously twitching his fingers.

"That f'la want me," he said, with resigned calm. "He take me back to jail." I looked at him. He was only about fifteen years of age. "Jail?" I thought. "How could a young bloke like that be in jail?"

The paddy wagon pulled up in front of us and a khaki-clad policeman walked up to us. He pointed to the young blackfellow and told him to get into the back of the paddy wagon. I decided to stick my neck out.

"What for?" I asked, in a brusque manner.

The police officer gave me a contemptuous look.

"He knows what for," he replied, looking at the frightened youth. "Don't you?" The lad lowered his head and nodded. The officer took a sheet of paper from his pocket and handed it to me. It was an arrest warrant. It appeared that the lad had escaped from Westbrook, which is a home — or rather, a penal home — for young offenders. The young black headed for the police wagon and, as he neared it, the officer gave him a rough push. The blood rushed to my head.

"Hey!" I yelled out loudly. "There's no need for that. He's going quietly. Christ! He's only a bloody kid." The police took no notice of me.

"I just want him to know who's boss, right from the start." So saying, he gave him another push into the wagon.

"You miserable bastard!" I could not stop my outburst, not thinking that he might toss me into his wagon too. Oddly enough, he took no notice of my abuse. Just at that moment, Ruby appeared from around the windmill and took in the scene immediately. She knew the young escapee and mildly berated him for running away from Westbrook and thereby making things much worse for himself and his parents. He hung his head and a tear dropped onto the dusty floor of the wagon. The police officer snickered as he locked the heavy wire door. He got behind the steering wheel and drove off in a cloud of dust.

The drama was over.

"Kill the bastards!"

I returned to Jack's camp after a few hours but not before buying a small bottle of instant coffee at the shop. When I arrived at the doorway, he was sitting at the table with a pencil and several pieces of paper.

"G'day Bill," he greeted me as I stood at the door. "I've been scribbling down a few notes as I thought of a few things. Come on in."

He spotted the bottle of coffee and, after a few "ahhhs", he busily scratched around and brought the fire back to life.

"That looks bloody good, Bill," he nodded towards the coffee which I placed on the table. "I'll soon get the water boiling."

He was very alert now. The little siesta had completely revived him. The billy began to bubble and I soon made the two mugs of coffee. Jack didn't comment, which made me wonder if he might have preferred his own bottlebrush brew. I asked him this.

"No, no," he said, anxiously. "That coffee'll do me. Bloody oath!" He spread the scrap of paper. "After you left this morning, I gave it a lot of thought. You know, what we've been talking about before."

"You didn't have a bit of sleep then?" I asked.

"Yes, I did," he replied. "I dozed off a bit. But then I

got to thinking about them things my father told me. I think better when I'm quiet. You remember when I was telling you about how that Telemon mob were camped on Christmas Creek?"

"Yes," I nodded. "I remember. But you didn't know how long they were there."

"That's right. I don't know, but I remember my father telling me that my grandfather said that they walked back towards Beenleigh. I remember him telling me that there was a group of those mounted black police camped somewhere around there." He gave a gummy smile and waited, I feel sure, to see how impressed I was with his memory and with this new information. I did not disappoint him. I remarked upon his very good memory. He smiled wider.

"But," I frowned at him, "why would they want to go near the police? I thought they were shit-scared of them."

"Yair, that's right, they were," Jack answered with a wink. "But they were going to get stuck into them. They reckon they could get rid of them in the night time."

"Get rid of them?"

"Kill the bastards! There was this white mongrel there, too. My father told me who it was but I've forgotten now."

It was, in fact, Lieutenant Wheeler. He was in the area in response to letters of complaint from a squatter, John Hardie, and others. Wheeler claimed later that, in the letter, Hardie had blamed the blacks for stealing sheep, and that Wheeler and his detachment were tracking the Telemons.[14]

"What happened?" I asked, anxiously. "Did they catch them?"

"No," he replied. "There was no one there. They

were probably out looking for my grandfather's mob. But they smashed the camp up a bit." Jack sat puffing heavily at the excitement of it all.

"They pissed off after that," he continued. "They didn't stop running until they were back in the Dugandan scrub." Old Cyclone Jack's eyes were darting around the tin shed as if looking for an escape route.

"Take it easy," I tried to calm him down a bit. He was a very excitable fellow. "Here, have some more coffee. There's stacks left." I shovelled two heaped spoonfuls into his mug and filled it up with, by now, lukewarm water.

"Aw, she'll be all right, Bill," he said, swamping the coffee down. "I get carried away a bit, you know."

"You're not wrong," I replied, laughingly.

He placed his mug down and turned his attention to the scraps of paper.

"It all comes back to me, you know," he said. "I can still see my father telling me all this thing."

"Will you tell me everything he told you?" I asked.

"If you reckon you've got the time."

"Plenty of time," I assured him. "I'll camp here again tonight if I have to."

"Does it mean that much to you?" he asked, screwing up his face.

"Yes, bloody oath," I answered. "That's what I came all the way up here for."

"What about Ruby? She want to go 'ome?"

"Ruby has looked after herself all her life," I said. "I think she will be able to care for herself for one night. Besides, she has some friends here. She's happy."

Jack nodded his head in approval. He finally finished his coffee, spitting the last mouthful onto the ground and pulling a face.

"Ah, well," he said, as he wiped his mouth with the

sleeve of his old dustcoat, "let's see, now. Where were we?"

"Buggered if I know," I replied. "You're the main actor. I think you said your grandfather's mob went back to the Dugandan scrub."

"Ah, yes, that's right." He looked closely at his scraps of paper.

"Now, my grandfather's tribe . . . listen, instead of calling them 'my grandfather's mob' all the bloody time, how about I just say 'the Telemons'?"

"If you like," I agreed. "It certainly would be less confusing."

"What's that mean?"

"Easier to understand."

"Mmm. Well, those Telemons weren't very happy in those scrubs because they could see the white bosses riding around. The gins used to go into the town sometimes to see what they could find out. But they had to be careful they weren't seen."

"Why not?" I asked. "Why wouldn't they want to be seen?"

Jack looked at me quickly. "Aw, no," he replied. "If those troopers seen 'em, they'd catch 'em and root 'em!"

"That's a bit crude, isn't it?" I remarked, trying not to smile at the look on Jack's face. "What town did they go into?"

"Fassifern," he answered. "You could see Fassifern from some parts of Dugandan scrub. 'Course, they didn't go into the town itself. Only the outside."

"Your mob must have been frightened, eh? How long did they stop there?"

"Well, they stay there for a while. But they often went down to the river."

"What river would that be, Jack?"

He thought for a while, twisting his beard around in his fingers.

"Aw, it must be the Logan," he guessed. "I remember my father telling me there was a lot of fish down at the Logan. Must be it."

"They would have caught plenty of other stuff there, too, wouldn't they? Kangaroos and that?"

"Nah," he answered vehemently. "Nothing there. All them white people chase 'em. They want all that grass. They put dogs on them. Hunt 'em to buggery."

I looked at him a little sceptically. I should not have because later, in Brisbane, I discovered many facts which backed up Jack's claims. In his *History of Australia,*[15] Mr Arthur W. Jose states:

> The blackfellow's life was a hard one . . . His tribe claimed a certain district for its hunting . . . this law, as may be imagined, caused much trouble between whites and blacks when the first settlers pushed their herds into the great plains; for the blackfellow could not at first understand why he (and they) may kill all the kangaroos he liked, but was punished for touching a bullock (white man's kangaroo). Settlers took up country without taking any account of the native's rights . . . demoralised by drink and the vices of meaner whites, some retreated into the more sterile interior as squatters occupied the better eastern lands . . . those who preferred to live their own lives grew more and more hostile as their hunting grounds were taken from them . . . the settlers in too many places, had taken the law brutally into their own hands. (p.107)

What Jose was trying to explain was the Aborigines' failure to understand why it was perfectly in order for the white man to kill as many kangaroos as he liked (black man's kangaroo), while the black man was punished for killing bullocks (white man's kangaroo). Aborigines had no conception of the monetary value of cattle. To their mind, it was just "good tucker" and plenty of it. Jose further states:

> The condition of the blacks on the coast has become a matter of some concern. Settlement has advanced upon the tribes so rapidly that they have lost their hunting grounds and have therefore been deprived of their only means of existence. The consequence has been the committal of depredations (spearing cattle and robbing huts &c.). While population was sparse, the large tracts of country were open to Aborigines . . . it was possible for the police to keep them back from settlements, but now, in driving them away from one occupied locality they were merely driven to another and so they are prevented from obtaining their natural food.

"Not only did they chase the roos away," Jack continued.

"No?" I replied, simply.

"They used poison on them, you know."

"What! The roos?"

"No. You silly bastard."

"I don't understand, Jack. Who poisoned who?"

"Well, those white settlers. They called them squatters. They the ones that did that."

Jack was becoming quite stirred again. I didn't want to calm him down because I was anxious to hear what he had to say. He was looking at me side-eyed. I didn't quite know what to do so I offered him a smoke. He accepted it and I applied a match for him.

"Jack," I ventured. "Just try and settle down a bit. Tell me about it."

He puffed the smoke and did, in fact, relax a little.

"Well, one day the tribe — the Telemons — they were all camped near a waterhole. A couple of gins saw these two blackfellas, you know, coming over the paddocks. They had a pack of something over their shoulders and they came up to the mob. They knew the mob — or the mob knew them, I don't know. They told them it was flour. Anyway, these two make a damper and start eating it. Pretty soon they get sick, sort of in pain, you know?" I nodded.

"Well, those two fella die in no time!"

"How the bloody hell did that happen? Where did they get it?"

Old Jack looked at me and grinned slyly.

"Aw," he replied. "That's what they done in those days. They used to put poison in some flour and give it to the blackfellas. Or else they'd leave it in a hut and the blackfellas would pinch it. Those squatter mongrels killed thousands of blackfellas like that."

I felt the skin on my cheeks crinkle and grow cold. Of course, I had heard of this practice but to be told, face to face, by one with personal knowledge was a new experience.

"When those blackfellas find out this thing, well, they make a bloody nuisance then."

Once again, Cyclone Jack's words proved correct. In 1861, a Select Committee on the Native Police Force was appointed. On Wednesday 14 May 1861, one of the witnesses, Captain John Coley, was questioned by the Chairman:

Q. You have seen a good deal of the Aborigines since your arrival?
A. Yes.
Q. What state were they in at the time of your arrival?
A. The Brisbane tribe at that time numbered about two hundred and fifty; that was about the number, at that time, of the tribe.
Q. Have they diminished since then?
A. They are all gone since then — they are all extinct. The present blacks are the offspring of the Ningey Ningey and Bribie Island tribes.
Q. Bribie Island?
A. Yes.

Q. You tell the Committee of your own knowledge of what the number of the tribe was on your arrival, that they have diminished since the settlement of the district?
A. Quite so. They are all gone, altogether extinct.

Q. Do you think that the establishment of the Native Police is an improvement on the old system of leaving settlers to protect themselves?
A. I believe it has been. On the Kilcoy Station, owned by Mr Evan Mackenzie, there were two white men killed, and an imported bull; and their retaliation was very severe on the blacks — they destroyed hundreds of them.
Q. In what way?
A. By shooting and poisoning them.
Q. What with?
A. With strychnine and arsenic, in flour.[16]

"They got the lot in the end," Jack was saying. "Trouble is, no one knows. They just don't know."

"Jack," I assured him, "I promise I will tell a great many people your story. A lot has already been told."

"Ah, yes, I know a lot has been told but how many people believe it?"

I pondered Jack's words. True; a lot of people did not believe the way it was. I think that is because people do not believe it *could* happen! Tales which have been bandied about did not seem to have that ring of truth about them. It was mere gossip. Just hearsay. No facts. Jack was bitter. I think his yarning with me over the last couple of days may have recalled an old and profound bitterness.

"Jack," I said to him. "It's been a long time since you've been with white people. Perhaps you might find things have changed."

He gave me a cynical grin. "It's not all that long since I've been down there, in that Brisbane," he informed me. "How was it that I couldn't get a bed for the night? I had to camp down at the river. I was going to camp in a park I came across, but Jeeeesus! There were all these blackfellas there drinking wine there. They were making such a big noise. Pissed, they were. I talked to one of them and he said a lot of them camp at the river. He said that a lot of police came to that park in the night-time. Even while I was talking to him I saw some police go past in a 'flash' car."

Jack was probably referring to Musgrave Park, a favourite meeting spot for Aborigines. He looked up at me for my reaction.

"You're lucky they didn't pick you up and toss you into jail," I said, jokingly.

Jack did not think it was very funny. He opened his eyes wide and looked at me. "Ooooo, fuck dat!" he shuddered. The thought of such an occurrence terrified him. He was speechless.

"Ah, I'm only joking, Jack." I tried to still his anxiety. "They wouldn't have chucked you in jail. They'd most likely have fed you to the ducks."

My lightheartedness had the desired effect. His face crinkled in a smile as he turned and looked at me.

"No, I know they wouldn't put me in jail," he lied. "I'll tell you, Bill, I liked those pies down there, I ate a lot of those."

He was back to normal again so I pressed on with my interview.

"Jack," I asked. "You said before that 'they got the lot in the end'. What did you mean?"

He thought for a moment. "Oh, that," he remembered. "Well, those blacktrackers caught that Telemon mob in the end. They caught them at that Dugandan place. Only a few got away. My grandfather was one of them. When the shooting started he grabbed my father and climbed up a tree and hid. It must have been a big fight, you know. When those Telemons took to the scrub, those troopers tied up their horses and chased them."

He threw his well-chewed butt onto the ground and pulled out his tobacco to roll another one. The dried tobacco was reduced to crumbs as he rolled it carefully into the paper.

"This weed is stuffed," he said. "The wind here dries every bloody thing." He managed to get the cigarette rolled and applied a match, taking care not to let his scraggy beard catch alight.

"There was another time, too," he said, nipping the end off his thin cigarette. "There was two of my grandfather's friends that was shot by those blacktrackers. They were on the way back to the camp and them troopers — ah, that's what they were called, troopers — they bailed them up and wanted to know where the camp was. Nobody knows what went on but, anyhow, one of them crawled back to the camp. He was lucky he got there because his guts was hanging out. He died after. The other was killed out in the paddock."

"Jack," I began. "How come so many blacks killed so many other blacks? I mean, why?"

He looked at me with a puzzled expression.

"What I mean is, if all the blacks had one common enemy — you know, the white man — why didn't all the blacks gang up together and fight that one common enemy? It just doesn't make bloody sense."

Cyclone Jack looked at me in silence for a while, screwing his face up and closing one eye as a sign that he knew I didn't understand about these things. He crossed back to his box seat and carefully sat down.

"Well, Bill," he explained, "those blacks that were made into troopers, they were brought up from as far as three hundred miles away, from a different area. They were different tribes, you know. They were not friendly with the local blackfellas here. They want to kill them and take the women." He dropped his shoulders in defeat. "You know, that's something the white man will *never* understand. Just because they're all black, that doesn't mean they're all mates."

During the time that Jack had been talking to me, he had not taken his cigarette out of his mouth. Now it was soaked with spittle and was on the point of disintegrating. I politely pointed this out to him and he removed the soggy butt and thipped bits of tobacco from his tongue.

"That's the trouble with me," he said. "I get onto something that upsets me and I get too excited."

"I don't blame you for getting excited, Jack," I consoled him. "I only hope I'm not causing you too much trouble by picking your brain about your grandfather."

"Nah," he replied. "As a matter of fact, it's good to get it off my chest."

It struck me as odd that, on the many occasions I have interviewed Aborigines who have bitter memories or have a story to tell about various occurrences, be it oppression, exploitation or, perhaps, some feeling of injustice they believe has been done to them, a common response has been that "it is good to get it off my chest" or "it's good to have a yarn about it".

"Jack," I asked. "Those two blacks who were killed, the ones you just told me about. Were they part of the Telemons?"

"Oh, those two," he said, after a moment. "Well, I think they — one of them, anyway — was supposed to be a witchdoctor; you know, Kadaitcha?"

At the mention of the word, "Kadaitcha", Jack lowered his voice and casually looked around behind him. I'm sure that if I had grabbed him and yelled, "Aahhhh!", he would have died of fright. The Kadaitcha custom is indelibly instilled into Aborigines, even today!

"And was he?" I enquired. "Was he a Kadaitcha?"

"Probably," he replied. "It seemed strange for two blackfellas to be away on their own like that. You know what I mean? Away from the tribe."

"Seems odd," I replied. "I suppose it was odd."

"Ah, well, that's how they worked, see," he explained. "See, those two might not have even belonged to the Telemon tribe. They could be from many miles away out, looking for 'payback'."

"What actually is 'payback'?" I asked. He cast his eyes around the tin hut, probably trying to think of some simple way to explain it to me.

"Well," he replied, "suppose a girl from some other tribe ran away with a boy from my grandfather's tribe. That's not allowed, you know. Well, those two will have to get punished. That might be by the Kadaitcha man or might be by the tribe. Might be that the Kadaitcha from both tribes will be after them. See, they after 'payback'."

"Yes, but what is 'payback'?" I asked again. "Is it revenge or punishment?"

"Well," Jack scratched his chin irritably, "it's sort of both. See, if one of the tribe get hurt or killed by another tribe, the Kadaitcha get 'payback'. Now, if one of the tribe do bad thing, then the Kadaitcha get 'payback'."

"So it's both?"

"Yes, I reckon both."

"Jack, if, as you say, two members of your tribe — a boy and a girl — ran away and they were not allowed to, what then? What would happen?"

"Ah, well, " Jack replied, making a twisting movement with his hands. "They'd be gone."

"Gone?"

"Yes. Either the Kadaitcha or the tribe would fix them up."

"How would they 'fix them up', Jack?" ("Fix them up"! What an expression!)

"Oh, well, they might get knocked on the head. They might be speared. Depends."

"And what about the Kadaitcha? Would they knock them on the head or spear them too?"

Before Jack answered, he looked outside the door. His eyes betrayed the seeming casualness of his action.

"No," he answered, satisfied there was no one around. "No, they don't do that sort of thing. They're trained. Those two people would be better off if they were taken back to their tribe, they'd stand a better chance."

"How is that, Jack?"

"Well, if they were punished by their tribe they might only be speared — or burned — and they might live. With that Kadaitcha, they'd have no chance at all." He looked at me quickly, furtively. "You've heard of 'singing', haven't you?"

"Singing? No. What's that?" I white-lied.

"Aw, shit," Jack spat. "I thought everybody knew that!"

"I've heard of this singing business but I'm buggered if I know what it means. Do they sing some sort of corroboree song, or what?"

"Well, you're a silly . . ." He stopped short.

I feel sure that if he had completed the sentence, it would have contained at least one expressive four-letter word. It was difficult to conceal my smile. Of course, I had heard of, and fully understood the Aboriginal custom of "singing". But I felt it important for *him* to tell *me* rather than to assume that the culture and customs of his father's tribe were no different from those of other tribes.

"Well," I replied in mock offence. "Singing is bloody singing to me."

Jack laughed, his beard parting to disclose an enormous mouth. "I'll tell you about it then, Bill." His nervousness had now left him. He no longer kept glancing out the door.

"Say you were the Kadaitcha man and you were after 'payback'. You'd go up to the blackfella that did the wrong thing and you'd hum softly — you don't sing at all. You hum some sort of . . . of . . . well, chant, I suppose you could call it. Now, the blackfella that done the wrong thing by the tribe . . . you know, he might have broken some sacred custom or something, he hears this hum because the Kadaitcha is right up close to him and looking fair at him. Nobody else hears it. This blackfella that hears it starts to pack the shits! He knows that the Kadaitcha man's curse is strong and he knows he is going to die. He's got to die. There's nothing he can to do to save himself now. It's too late now. See, he's been brought up with that custom and he might have seen it happen to other people."

"But can't he say to himself, 'This thing is all a lot of bullshit'?" I argued.

"No bloody fear," Jack laughed. "It will play on his mind so much that he will talk himself into dying. Strange, eh?" He was looking at me intently.

"Just you make sure you don't start humming at me, old mate," I teased.

"Aw, no," he half-laughed. "I couldn't do that. You've got to be trained."

"Jack, what about this 'pointing the bone' caper? What's it all about?"

"Ah, that's different," he replied, lighting another smoke. He puffed furiously before continuing. "That's totally different. See, that's a funny thing that; pointing the bone, as you call it."

"I can't imagine it to be very funny," I remarked. "It still kills people, doesn't it?"

"In a different way," he explained. "People that get boned can get it out if they're smart, or lucky."

He seemed to hold his breath, waiting for me to ask the obvious question. I did not disappoint him.

"How?" I asked. "How could you get away from it if one of those Kadaitcha men boned you?"

For reply, he threw out his bony chest. "I was boned once." He slid his eyes in my direction, making sure that I was suitably impressed.

"I thought I was a dead man for a while," he continued. "Some of my friends took me to a white doctor. He gave me tablets but they didn't do any good. They couldn't find out what was wrong with me. I told them I might be boned but they told me, 'Bullshit'."

I watched as he pulled the grubby dustcoat aside to expose a set of bony ribs. He screwed his head around, trying to look at a spot below the ribcage.

"Somewhere there." He touched his ribs and I saw a definite raised scar. I ran my finger over it and felt the hardened skin.

"OK," I said, trying to be unimpressed. "What happened?"

Once more he waited before he replied. But he could contain himself no longer. "Well, when I was a young fella," he blurted out, "I did the wrong thing to another man's wife. It wasn't my fault, you know," he added quickly.

"Sure, sure," I harassed him jokingly. "It never is your fault. Go on, tell me the load of bullshit!"

Old Jack curled up, squealing with delight as he realised that I, too, am a man who could probably tell him a similar story.

"No, no. It's true," he insisted, trying to control his glee. "The trouble began when her husband came back before it was over."

Once again he doubled up with laughter. He laughed so hard that, because of his croaky old throat, no sound came except a harsh expulsion of smoky air. I was also helpless with laughter but my amusement was caused mostly by the impossible sounds coming from Jack's throat.

"Ah, the capers I got up to when I was young," he bragged. "I was a wild one in my day."

"I daresay," I concurred. "But what happened? I'll bet when you got boned it wasn't too bloody funny." My remark sobered him up somewhat.

"Well, it wasn't 'til months later — could be four or five months later — when I started to feel crook," he explained. "I wasn't spewy or anything like that. I just felt off and I seemed to be getting weak. Then, one day I went down and I couldn't get up. I was too weak. I couldn't eat or drink anything. All I could do was feel tired all the time. Then one day an old drover from Lake Nash [a cattle station in the Northern Territory] got off his horse and came over to me. I was lying under a tree. He stood looking at me for a while, then he said, 'You bin caught eh?' I shook my head and told him I wasn't but he reckon I was. He pressed my back and, gees, it hurt like buggery." Jack winced at the memory.

"He told me to roll over but I couldn't move, I was so weak. He rolled me over on my guts and did something with a stick he had in his saddlebag. Next thing I know there was blood everywhere. All over his hands too. I tried to look what was happening but he had my head between his legs. Gees! All that blood." He shivered slightly and wound the old dustcoat around him and tucked the ends into his trousers. He fiddled around idly with the rope which served as a belt.

"Go on," I urged, impatiently. "Then what happened? How long did it take before you felt better?"

"Straight away," he croaked. "I just got straight up and I was OK. That man was an old Kadaitcha man, for sure. I could smell it."

"Smell it?"

"Aw, yes," he said, earnestly. "They got a certain smell. My oath."

"How many married women have you stuffed around with since then?" I asked him, jocosely. "Did it teach you a lesson?" He tried to hide his smile by turning away and wiping his mouth with his dustcoat.

"You cunning old bastard," I laughed. His grin widened.

"Jack," I asked him, after a while. "Does that boning business work on white people in the same way as it works on blacks?

He thought for a moment. "Nah," he replied. "Only a blackfella can get caught."

"Caught? Is that what you call it?"

"Mainly. Most people call it that, but some say, 'He bin boned, that f'la'. See, it's blackfella culture to believe that training when they young." He paused, waiting to see if I was listening with the attention he expected. Satisfied that I was grasping the edge of my seat, his voice took on a solemn note. He leaned closer to me, inviting me to join him in the mystery.

"This boning is a serious business, you know," he

informed me. "It is about the one thing that the blackfella fears most. They don't joke about it. Even now, out on the stations, if a strange blackfella turns up, they get frightening. Bloody oath."

"But I thought blacks took a more modern view of those things in this day and age," I offered.

"No. That's not right," he assured me. "It's bred into them. They believe these things. It's part of their culture. I know many times about a blackfella bin boned. Make you frightened." He screwed up his eyebrows and looked up at the smoke-blackened ceiling. "As a matter of fact," he resumed his story, "it wasn't that long ago that a strange blackfella came here to Urandangie. He just passed through and a lot of people here got frightened of him. Not only here, but further up, too, in Mt Isa."

He looked around again and peered outside with widening eyes. The old man was actually frightening himself with his tale about the Kadaitcha.

In my experience of speaking with Aborigines and touching on the subject of the Kadaitcha, the informant, after relating a personal experience or an experience he had witnessed, usually ended up quite shaken, so firmly established was the belief. Apart from "boning" and "singing", there are other ways in which the Kadaitcha may bring about the desired effect. One common yet strangely little known practice was the use of "death powder" which the Aborigines called, "Maoriormoyari". This was most commonly used by the local Urandangie tribe, the *Jaroinga*. This death powder seemed to be white ashes and was placed near the victim. The most common method was to place the substance under his blanket or sleeping mat. It was considered to be pretty potent stuff and the person who handled it took great care not to let it touch him. It was usually applied with a shell or a stick. Another nasty device was a small, sharp emu bone, called a Chirooko, about three inches in length. The purpose of this little gem was to bring about the rotting of the genitals. It could be used in either of two ways. It could be stuck into the ground close to where the intended victim evacuated or placed inside the possum skins he used as a blanket. (Of course, it was many years before Aborigines realised that venereal disease was a disease brought in by the Europeans.)

Jack remained silent for many minutes. I did not disturb his thoughts as his vacant gaze told me his thoughts were far away. He eventually returned to a normal state, the wildness fading from his eyes as he turned and looked at me once more.

"You know," he said, seriously, "that Wheeler mongrel was never found." His thoughts had returned to the Native Mounted Police.

"What are you talking about?" I enquired.

"He was charged with murdering a kid. I think it was Rockhampton, and he never showed up at that court.[17] He's never been found." He winked knowingly to me.

"What do you reckon happened to him?"

"A lot of people say that the Kadaitcha got him. I think that's right, too. My father reckon that's what happened."

"Was that the general opinion back in the days of your grandfather?"

He peered at me beneath his bushy eyebrows. "Well, what do you reckon? He was put up for killing a blackfella, so he must have been a bad bastard."

"What would have happened to Wheeler if the tribe got hold of him?"

"Skin 'im," Jack answered immediately.

My toes curled! What a thought. I wanted to get off that subject.

"When did your father die?" I asked, rather crudely.

He thought for a while, pulling a face, before answering. "Aw, about thirty years ago, I suppose," he replied.

"How old was he, do you know?"

"About sixty or so."

It has been my observation in the past that times, dates and ages mean very little to the tribal Aborigines. It was with this in mind that I did not pay too much attention to Cyclone Jack's reply. However, after making some calculations based on historical events, it would seem that Jack's father would have been, roughly, about five years of age at the time of the Dugandan massacre. He may have died in 1920 and Jack may have been born around the turn of the century. I reasoned that Jack was about eighty-five when I spoke with him in that hot, forlorn, dusty paddock on the outskirts of Urandangie.

He stood up; he had had enough. He removed his old dustcoat and walked out the door and headed for a clump of shady trees a little way off. Once there, he spread the dustcoat on the ground and slowly, ever so slowly, he lowered himself down. I imagined that he would now reflect on his fading memories; memories which, throughout his simple and meagre life, must have sparked more than a little hatred of the white man. Old Jack moved slowly and painfully onto his side and tried to settle his hip into the unyielding ground.

"They must all suffer"

As I sat watching Jack resting on the ground in the shade of the trees, my thoughts recalled the story he had related to me during the previous few hours. I conjured up visions of what that attack at the Dugandan scrub must have been like:

> As the attack began, the blue smoke of burnt gunpowder would have drifted up through the stillness of the Dugandan scrub. It would have wafted downwind, flaring the nostrils of the stamping, frightened horses as they pulled at the reins, trying to break free from the saplings to which they were tethered. The birds would have flown away at the sounds of the first gunshots, the possums would have crawled deeper into their hollow trees and a goanna might have been clutching the far side of a tree, nervously flicking its tongue, as though trying to taste the safety of the situation. The terrified screams of the dying blacks would have frightened the wonga pigeons into the deepest recesses of the scrub. Finally, the scrub would return to quietness. The black members of the Queensland Native Police Force would have returned to their Commandant, sweat running down their naked bodies, following the tracks of scratches made by wait-awhile vines and the thorny trunks of sassafras trees at the height of the slaughter. The cruel twist of Lieutenant Frederick Wheeler's mouth would convey to his troopers, "Well done".

But there was one sound still remaining in the Dugandan scrub. It was the sound of a throbbing heart which came from high up in a hoop pine tree. Up there, on one of the topmost branches and hidden by the dark green foliage, sat old Cyclone Jack's grandfather, clutching his young son to his side. After the first confrontation with the murderous troopers, he had raced through the scrub and, spotting the pine tree just beyond a high rock, he had scooped up his child and, after scrambling up the rock, made a desperate leap for the lower branches. Then, his belly flattened against the blind side, he watched in horror as the remainder of his tribe — the Telemons — were annihilated. He would have watched as the last tribesman fell; the last muscle spasm faded to stillness; the final twitch of a black slender finger.

I rinsed my mug in the bucket of cloudy water, picked up my cigarettes and headed for my vehicle.

During my interviews with Cyclone Jack, his constant reference to Wheeler, although vague, was very interesting. Perhaps at this stage of my narrative, I should inform the reader as to what manner of man he was. It is well documented that he was a cruel and merciless officer of the Native Police.

Wheeler was promoted to Second Lieutenant on 7 December 1857. During his tour of duty in the Port Curtis area, under Lieutenant John Murray, it seemed that right from the beginning of his career, his brutality was manifest. His edict of "shoot them . . . kill them all" made him, perhaps, the most feared man in the Native Mounted Police Force.

At the completion of a tour of duty in the Mount Larcom district in central Queensland, he submitted a report to his superior. It reads, in part: "It was too late in the evening to do any good but next morning overtook them but was not able to shoot any as they had already crossed the river." He did, however, manage to take six gins prisoner! Further on in his report he added: "They must all suffer, for the innocent must be held responsible for the guilt of others." [18]

Wheeler was later transferred to Headquarters at Sandgate, which had been established in 1854 as a result of an attack on Tom Dowse and his family, the first settlers in that area.

Wheeler's barbarous nature was exposed during the Select Committee enquiry on 3 May 1861. In the following series of questions taken from the transcript, he is being questioned by the Chairman, the Honourable R.R. MacKenzie:

Q. Do you remember the affair at Coochin in December last?
A. Nothing took place at Coochin; it was near Dugandan.
Q. Were you sent for upon that occasion?
A. Yes, I received four or five letters from settlers — Mr Henderson, Mr Compigné, Mr Hardie and others — telling me that the blacks had been robbing the huts, stealing the sheep, and threatening the shepherds. Mr Compigné had left part of his run on that account, and brought the sheep to the head station.
Q. Did you go up there with your detachment?
A. I went up directly I received the letters to Mr Compigné's station on the Logan.
Q. Where is Dugandan?
A. On the Teviot Brook.
Q. What did you do when you came from Mr Compigné's station?
A. I went first to Mr Compigné's and from that to where the Albert runs into the Logan, but I did not find any blacks there. I then went over to the sea-coast, and followed it down to Point Danger. Finding no tracks there, I went over the mountains back again to Compigné's, and thence to Telemon; followed up Christmas Creek till I came underneath McPherson's Range and Mount Lindsay. I found the tracks underneath the ranges there, heading towards the large Dugandan scrub, between the Ten-mile and Fifteen-mile station. I found the blacks in the large Dugandan scrub.

Q. What did you do then?
A. I dispersed them.
Q. How did you know they were the blacks who committed the outrages?
A. I followed their tracks for a fortnight.
Q. Had you any other evidence — were any of them recognized by wearing clothes or blankets?
A. They were all naked.
Q. How many of them were there?
A. The camps extended for about three miles; there were several different tribes; they had been congregating there for some time. They usually come down there before Christmas time; it is on the high road to Ipswich, between that and the salt water.
Q. Had you any direct evidence to shew that they were the blacks who had committed the outrages complained of?
A. The shepherds at Mr Compigné's told me that the blacks had come down from the Telemon side of the range.
Q. Had they been by the Bunya scrub?
A. No.
Q. Did they make any resistance?
A. I only dispersed the Telemon mob.
Q. Not the whole of them?
A. No, none of the others.
Q. What led you to disperse the Telemon blacks?
A. They always do the mischief; the same mob had been robbing Mr Collins's station at Telemon.
Q. Were there any warrants out against those blacks?
A. No. Warrants are never given out against the blacks for cattle-stealing, which is done by the whole tribe.
Q. Did you recognize any of them?
A. It was getting dark, but I recognized two or three of them.
Q. Had you any information to prove that they were the same blacks who robbed Mr Collins's station?
A. No. I only know from what the shepherds told me, that a certain tribe of blacks committed the depredations, and that they had headed towards the sea-coast.

Q. At the time of this affray the troopers were out of your sight?
A. Yes, they were out of my sight for about half-an-hour.

Q. Do those troopers understand English sufficiently to comprehend your orders?
A. Oh, yes.
Q. Did you give them orders to go into the scrub?
A. Yes.
Q. What was the nature of those orders?
A. I told them to surround that camp of Telemon blacks, and to disperse them.
Q. What do you mean by dispersing?
A. Firing at them. I gave strict orders not to shoot any gins. It is only sometimes, when it is dark, that a gin is mistaken for a blackfellow, or might be wounded inadvertently.
Q. Do you think it is a proper thing to fire upon the blacks in that way?
A. If they are the right mob, of which I had every certainty.

Q. What are the general orders of your Commandant?
A. It is a general order that, whenever there are large assemblages of blacks, it is the duty of an officer to disperse them. There are no general orders for these cases; officers must take care that proper discretion is exercised.

Q. Don't you consider this is a very loose way of proceeding — surrounding blacks' camps, and shooting innocent gins?
A. There is no other way.[19]

There was not the slightest trace of mercy in Wheeler's soul. Indeed, his practice of undue severity on his own black troopers had caused a detachment of twelve men to desert him.

During the Select Committee enquiry the three Aborigines, whom Cyclone Jack had told me were shot and partially burnt in Hardie's paddock, were mentioned, a fact which proved that his recall had been deadly accurate. The three blacks who were shot were the survivors of Wheeler's attack on the camp. Wheeler claimed that only two were shot but later evidence proved this to be incorrect. Wheeler was further questioned about the incident by the Committee Chairman:

Q. What number of blacks were killed on that occasion?
A. Two.
Q. Did you see the dead bodies?
A. Yes.
Q. Was not one of them an old man?
A. A middle-aged man.
Q. Had he grey hair?
A. Not particularly so.
Q. Were you with the Police then?
A. Yes.
Q. With your troopers?
A. Yes. I dispersed that mob on account of having received a letter from Mr Hardie, stating that a mob of blacks had been threatening him, and that he could not get rid of them.
Q. Had they been spearing Mr Hardie's cattle?
A. He said they had been spearing the cattle at Moograh and threatening the lives of the men.
Q. In fact, you saw nothing yourself?
A. No, I could not waste time to see whether a cow or a bullock had been speared.[20]

This evidence proved Wheeler's unwillingness to seek proof of depredations as claimed by various squatters. This seems an odd procedure for an experienced police officer well versed in the necessity of proof as evidence of a crime. His evidence impressed nobody, least of all the leading newspaper, the *Courier*. The editor was quite cutting in his editorial:

> One solitary reply of Lieutenant WHEELER'S explains the whole matter, and affords a clue to the intentions of those who wish to maintain the Native Police Force in existence. In answer to a question as to whether the gentleman named (Compigné) was with him on a particular occasion, that officer replied, "*No, I never take any white people with me*". Who can hear of such a statement as this without following it to its issue? If Lieutenant WHEELER never acts otherwise than he is entitled to act by virtue of his office, why object to the presence of whites? Simply because of this, Lieutenant WHEELER knows well enough the work of the force is *extermination*.

The editorial went on to explain that, to carry out this extermination successfully, it was important that "any person whose evidence might be accepted in a court of law, must not witness the murder and butchery which took place during a 'dispersal' because a 'hempen necklace' [noose] *might* be the reward of an arch-perpetrator".[21]

On 8 May 1861, Dr Henry Challinor was called in to the Select Committee enquiry for examination. Challinor was the Coroner for Ipswich. He was also the Magistrate. It was he who, in his capacity as Coroner, examined the bodies on Hardie's property. He viewed the Select Committee with polite contempt, as did many others. He was questioned by the Chairman:

Q. You are the Coroner of the Police District of Ipswich?
A. I am.
Q. I find that on the third and fourth of January last year you instituted a Magisterial Enquiry at Fassifern respecting the death of some blacks — did you hold a Magisterial, and *not* a Coroner's Inquest then, or did you on any subsequent occasion?
A. I held a Magisterial Enquiry on the third of January — an enquiry commencing on the third, and adjourned to the fourth, and subsequently to other dates, which I can't remember just now, but the date was put to each of the depositions.

Q. Now, with regard to what happened at Fassifern — you received certain information, and proceeded to act upon it?
A. I did.
Q. Will you state what you saw — what came under your own observation?
A. I observed three dead blackfellows — one of the bodies was considerably burned; two of them I recognized as being old men, because they were grey-headed — one in particular had a grey beard.

Q. There were three, I think you stated?
A. There were three . . .
Q. Did you notice any particular wounds in the bodies of these blacks?
A. The skulls of two of them had been fractured, and there were what appeared to be bullet wounds on the body.
Q. Do you consider that the evidence brought before you was sufficiently conclusive to warrant you in assuming that Lieutenant Wheeler was the cause of death in the case of these blacks?
A. I do.

Q. You have stated in your letter to the Attorney-General that "the shooting of the said blacks is now distinctly and unequivocally traced to Lieutenant Wheeler, and the detachment of Native Police under his command, on the 24th day of December last". I now ask you, how have you come to that conclusion?
A. From the depositions — the sworn depositions.[22]

Like many other interested (and somewhat amused) people who followed the course of the unfolding performance, Challinor recognised it for the farce it was. Instead of allowing the witnesses to tell their account in their own way, the inquisitors put leading questions to them, or, as the *Courier*'s editor so succinctly put it:

> Had the hon. gentleman [Chairman MacKenzie who, incidentally, was the Colonial Treasurer] been a retained Barrister of doubtful attainments, he could not have done the work better than he did, and he would have deserved a *douceur* at the hands of his employers for his skill in propounding "leading questions":[23]

"There were three, I think . . ."[24]
"Don't you think . . . they are deceitful, treacherous and false?"[25]
"Have you never been brought into collision with the blacks, from their depredations?"[26]

"Did you not say . . . that Mr Hardie said his bullocks had been speared and hunted by the blacks?"[27]

And so the farce went on. Even before the Committee sat, the newspapers saw through the sham:

> We cannot congratulate the House upon their choice of a Select Committee to enquire into the organization and management of the Native Police Force, and into the recent charges which have, from more than one quarter, been made against that troop. The Committee was, it is true, chosen by ballot, but we all know how entirely one-sided, by a little previous concert and combination, committees so chosen can occasionally be formed . . . we feel inclined to ask what amount of impartiality in calling witnesses, taking evidence, and framing a report, can be expected from a committee composed of Messrs. MACKENZIE, FITZSIMMONS, GORE, MOFFATT, BLAKENEY, ROYDS, WATTS, and FERRETT . . . a more one-sided selection could not have been made, and we cannot exonerate the government from the blame attachable to that selection, as they possessed the power to prevent it had they chosen to exert themselves to do so.[28]

Obviously, the newspapers of that era were quite fearless.

So as not to shirk their duty to the reading public, the *Courier* severely criticised the Committee report:

> The strictures we passed upon the composition of the Committee at the time of its appointment have been fully borne out, and although each member of the house who was connected with it would doubtless vehemently assert his innocence of partiality, and protest that he was perfectly unbiased in his judgment, we are only bound to take the asseverations of each hon. member for what they may be worth. A more piquant farce was never enacted. It is excruciatingly funny to witness the apparent solicitude of the Chairman for the souls of the Aborigines, and to see how cleverly each member of the Committee extracted as much as he wanted from the doubtful witnesses and no more . . .[29]

The paper quoted one witness who claimed that the "inquisitors" knew, in advance, what questions to ask so that the reply could only be favourable to the enquiry.

Indeed, the Committee's report was incomplete, as the evidence of some of the witnesses was not included and it is left to readers to draw their own conclusions as to whether this was an attempt to conceal some of the facts relating to the murder of blacks on Hardie's station. For instance:

> Edward Quinn, being duly sworn, stated — I am Chief Constable of the Ipswich police force. I was present when Henry Challinor, Esq., J.P., requested Dr Lucas, on the evening of the 2nd instant (January), to accompany him to Fassifern to attend a magisterial inquiry respecting the death of three aboriginals who were then lying dead in the scrub adjoining the head station, Fassifern; Dr Lucas said, "I cannot go there to-night for I have only just returned from there, and my horse is knocked up. If I had known you were going up I would not have come down. While I was there I told Mr Hardie that there was a report that some blacks had been shot there, and that Dr Challinor would be going up to hold an inquest upon them, and Mr Hardie replied that there would be no inquest there, for there had been no blacks shot." This conversation was addressed to Dr Challinor.[30]

The evidence of Dr Lucas was omitted from the Committee Report as was that of Sergeant Carson: "Sergeant Carson's evidence, it will be seen, on reference, contains a plain story of the way in which Mr Hardie endeavoured to baffle him in an attempt to serve a summons on Bennett."[31]

Hardie fiddled with the truth by saying that Bennett was not in his employ. It was incongruous that Bennett just happened to be the overseer in the employ of Mr John Ferrett, MLA, who was the owner of Wallann Station. Ferrett was one of the inquisitors on the Select Committee on the Native Police Force! Of course, most of the station owners were mates, not only with each other, but also with the officers of the Native Mounted Police. Indeed, Lieutenant Wheeler's wife was spending Christmas at Coochin Station, owned by one of the witnesses, Mr Leonard Lester.[32]

Later in his evidence, Dr Challinor related an amazing incident which bore out the accuracy of Cyclone Jack's story. As the reader may remember, Jack's father "always had a wonky arm". Challinor is being questioned by Mr Moffatt, a member of the Select Committee:

> Q. Was any allusion made yesterday to the affray at Dugandan?
> A. I was asked some questions about it, but I do not recollect what they were.
> Q. Do you recollect how many bodies were found there upon that occasion?
> A. It was said there were two, but I only found one.
> Q. What was the appearance presented by that body?
> A. It was injured, evidently by gun-shot wounds. I may say that besides those killed there were other blacks wounded.
> Q. Did you see them?
> A. Yes; I attended one of them who had received a gun-shot wound. In one case, a bullet appeared to have glanced round the rib, and come out at the shoulder blade, or else penetrated the chest . . . and the ball grazed the child's shoulder. That man recovered.[33]

There is probably little doubt, given the place, the time and the expert evidence of Dr Challinor, that the black who received the wound in the chest was Jack's grandfather and the child whom he had held in his arms was Jack's father.

One of the most satisfying rewards in the life of an historian is when oral histories can be corroborated by recorded history, particularly faded and enigmatic events which took place more than 125 years ago. When Cyclone Jack told me of his grandfather's experiences in 1860, I was, indeed, sceptical. Well, perhaps not really sceptical, but certainly I had an open mind.

Actually, very little information was recorded of the murder and acts of violence perpetrated on such an enormous scale by the Native Mounted Police. While it was the duty of the officer-in-charge to keep account of deceased Aborigines, nonetheless, as has been borne out by the evidence of the Select Committee, orders and instructions given to the officers of the Native Mounted Police were couched in very cloaked terms indeed. For instance, when attempting to apprehend fleeing blacks, the black troopers were required to call out the words, "Surrender in the Queen's name". How ridiculous! What would a tribal blackfellow know about such subtleties? Of course, when the blacks continued their flight of terror, the patrolling detachment had licence to shoot them down under the flimsiest legal cover. The statement in Henry Lamond's book *Native Mounted Police* gives an insight into anti-black mentality:

> It is not intended to give details of any punishments, massacres, raids or deeds of violence. Those men [settlers] lived in a rough age; they had to hand out ready and rough justice; they had to adapt themselves to the mental levels of the Aborigines with whom they lived. They did it. They made the country safe for generations to follow.[34]

Bullets and poison were not the only killers to the black population. Many Aborigines were hanged, both in the bush and in the town of Brisbane. Perhaps the most ghastly incident took place in Brisbane on 5 January 1855. I allude, of course, to the bungled hanging of one Aborigine known as Dundalli, convicted for killing white timber workers in the vicinity of the Pine River. He was hanged in the centre of Brisbane, but not before many hundreds of Aborigines were herded into the township by native police and forced to watch the spectacle of "white man's justice"![35]

But the hangman had misjudged the length of the rope and made it too long. Dundalli plunged to the ground. The fall did not kill him and he lay struggling until the executioner raced forward and before a horrified audience lifted his legs off the ground and held them up so that his neck took the full weight of his body until he choked to death. White man's justice had not only been done — it was certainly seen to be done on that occasion!

Cyclone Jack had often said to me that "blackfellas were blamed for a lot of things, most of them were wrong because they were only getting 'payback' ". It has been documented many times that most black "atrocities" were actually caused by the white man himself. His greed, his lust, his deceit and his ignorance of tribal laws and customs have often generated a vengeful reaction from blacks. Perhaps one of the most notorious reactions was the attack on Hornet Bank Station, not far from the town of Taroom, on 27 October 1857. Cyclone Jack would have classified this attack as "payback". Enquiries and extensive research have pinpointed particular incidents which triggered the attack.[36] They involved the violation of tribal laws and customs, in particular the violation of gins.[37]

It was an officer with the Native Police Force, Sublieutenant Thomas Ross, who initially brought a number of blacks onto Hornet Bank Station, claiming they would make excellent workers. And so they were. All went very well until the Native Police began seducing the gins. The Fraser boys themselves were not without blame:

> By mid-1857 the abuse of Jiman lubras by the troopers and the Fraser boys had reached a peak. Not only were the Native Police troopers taking the Jiman women by force, but the whites at Hornet Bank were allowing them to do so. In addition, the shepherds on the Upper Dawson stations were guilty of this practice, *which also extended to the Fraser men themselves.*[38]
>
> Martha Fraser was aware of the situation; she had repeatedly asked Nicoll [Lieutenant Francis Nicoll, Native Mounted Police officer], when visiting the Dawson, to reprove her sons *for forcibly taking the "young maidens"*, telling Nicoll that she expected harm to come of it. They were in the habit of doing this, she said, notwithstanding her entreaties to the contrary. Among the working men in the area *the Frasers were "famous for the young gins"*. It is not surprising, then, that at this time, the desire to become one of the committers of rape was very intense among the blacks of Upper Dawson.[39]

An incident was to occur which further aggravated the situation. A black had been found with rations usually supplied to white workers. When questioned as to how they came to be in his possession, the black replied that he had exchanged the favours of his gin with a white man to obtain the rations. This explanation was not believed and he was shot dead on the spot. Outraged blacks decided, in response to this "last straw", to attack the station; the Fraser family, most of whom were innocent, were the victims.

The day prior to the attack on Hornet Bank passed quietly. The usual activity connected with station life wound down at dusk. Historian Gordon Reid vividly characterises the scene:

> The day had been unusually hot for the season and the evening air was full of breezeless semi-tropical languor. The cicadas had ceased their noise and the cry of the curlew and the hoot of the mopoke in the distance were the only sounds from the bush. The moon was already high as the sun had gone down; now at its first quarter, it would offer adequate illumination for persons moving through the ironbark, cypress pines, Moreton Bay ash

and bauhinia surrounding the station. The Frasers had gone to bed early.[40]

And then, minutes after dawn . . . holocaust!

The blame for the attack on Hornet Bank — or, rather for allowing the attack to take place — was sheeted home to Second Lieutenant Thomas Ross for his "inefficiency" in patrolling the Dawson area. The charge stated, in effect, that were he not such an "inefficient officer" and had he contained his detachment "under proper control", the Hornet Bank affair would never have happened. However, on closer inspection, this accusation must be discounted. Ross had been suspended on 7 September — seven weeks *before* the attack! The letter advising Ross of his suspension was dated and signed by the Commandant, Edric Morisset, during a tour of inspection in the Dawson district, and Ross was not aware that he had been suspended until he received the letter on 20 September when he returned from patrol.

Ross had taken singular exception to Morisset's accusation and had appealed to Alfred Denison, the private secretary to the Governor-General.[41] The appeal had been passed to Captain John Wickham, the Government Resident, who, because of pressing business in Brisbane, in turn instructed Lieutenant John Murray, Ross's area Commandant, to enquire into the affair. Murray had written to several pastoralists, seeking their general opinion of Ross.[42] Their replies were both favourable and unfavourable. One (Miles) replied that he had no charge of neglect of duty to make about Ross. Andrew Scott asserted in his reply that he had always found him ready and willing to do his duty. Two other pastoralists, John Scott and William Thomson, assured Murray that Ross had no charge to answer. They further assured him that Ross applied himself to his duties and was only too willing to respond to a call for assistance, and also remarked that Ross was quite competent in keeping a detachment of troopers under control. He was entitled to great consideration and credit.[43]

The replies to Murray's questionnaire were forwarded to the Colonial Secretary, *except the favourable replies from pastoralists such as Miles, Scott and Thomson*. It was on the strength of the *unfavourable* replies that Morisset had assumed licence to suspend Ross. But, as already stated, that had been seven weeks before the Hornet Bank attack. Notwithstanding, after requests to the Colonial Secretary for copies of the deprecatory letters were refused, Ross was dismissed from the Force on 19 March 1858. Yet throughout all the reports and other written evidence, one vital fact in Ross's favour failed to emerge — Ross did not have a detachment with him. All he had was one man and one boy!

That avenue of blame now exhausted, the usual righteous and convenient reasons for the attack were namely the barbarity and malevolence of the crude, uncivilised blacks. White reprisals were swift and callous. Men, women and children were killed — including three gins who were shot in the back and left decomposing on squatter's runs. It has been claimed that when the guns stopped smoking more than four hundred blacks had perished!

"I ran like hell!"

Later in the afternoon I wandered over to Jack's tin shed mainly, I think, to scrounge another mug of coffee. As I neared the building I casually gazed over to where he had bedded down to rest several hours earlier. He was still lying out there, his hands clasped under his head forming a makeshift pillow. On hearing my approach he twisted his shaggy head in my direction. Recognising me, he scrambled awkwardly to his feet and stood swaying and blinking his eyes.

"By hell," he said, brushing clouds of dust from his hair. "I must have had a good sleep there, you know."

"I'm buggered if I know how you can sleep in this bloody heat," I remarked.

"Aw, it's not too bad here in the shade," he replied. "I must have been pretty tired, I reckon."

We walked over to the shed and Jack fussed about, trying to get the fire to burn. He had no hope. The cleverest blackfellow in Australia would not have been able to coax life from those dead ashes. There was no kindling left and the only wood in the shed would have been suitable for railway sleepers!

"Hang on a minute, Jack," I said, walking over to the Datsun. "I've got a bottle of petrol in the back. I'll get the bastard going." I returned with the petrol and gathered a few twigs. I set the fire and poured some of the petrol onto it. I stood back to toss the match. Jack let out with a startled yell and cowered against the wall.

"Watch out," he warned. "I nearly blew my arse off like that once." I had not, of course, poured on much petrol and the fire started with a small, but lively "whoosh". The yellow in the whites of Jack's eyes shone as he looked sideways at my actions. Satisfied that we were not going to be blown up, he busied himself by placing sticks in vital places and soon the fire settled down to a nice steady flame. Jack filled the battered old billy can with the cloudy water.

"She'll soon be boiling," he said. I was anxious to have another conversation with him like the one about the Native Mounted Police we'd had earlier in the day. I felt sure he had a lot more interesting tales to tell me and I wanted to record them. However, during the afternoon I had gingerly taken the tape recorder to pieces, in order to clean out the fine white dust which had caused it to cease operating the previous day. I found the task of dismantling the thing quite easy, but it was a different matter getting all the bits to fit where I thought they should fit! Of course the result was that I had a stuffed-up tape recorder and several loose bits. I silently hoped my vehicle would not break down as well! Jack placed a pannikin of coffee — fresh coffee — onto the rickety table and rubbed his gums together as he sipped it.

"Well," I prompted. "What are we going to talk about today?"

"Aw, bugger if I know," he replied. "You think of something."

This invitation assured me that Jack, indeed, wanted to tell me more stories.

"Jack," I asked, after finishing off my coffee, "did you ever hear of the Queensland Aboriginal Act?"

"Aw, yes," he answered immediately. "I knew about it but I didn't worry about it. I took no notice." He looked at me with what I interpreted as a defiant stare. To amplify his words, he spat on the ground. "I never let it worry me. When I looked like getting into trouble I just pissed off."

"Did you get into trouble?" I enquired.

"Once," was his brief reply.

"Well, tell me about it," I urged. "What happened?"

"Got any of them smokes left?" he rubbed his hands together in the characteristic Aboriginal "Got a smoke?" gesture. I took out my packet of cigarettes and tossed it onto the table. He leaned over, carefully balancing his flimsy box seat, took one out and lit it.

"Now, about the Act," I probed. "What happened?"

"You know, it happened a long time ago," he began. "I was just a young fella. I was walking along the road near the Pine River — that's way down south — and some white bloke came along and told me that I had to go and work on his property."

"Was it a cattle property?" I asked.

"Aw, yes," Jack replied, making a half-circle with his arm. "Bloody big place. I don't know what it's called now. I used to know but I've forgotten. S'posed to have thousands of cattle there."

"What happened? Did you work on his station?"

Jack sniggered a little, no doubt reliving that chain of events.

"No bloody fear," he replied, shaking his head vigorously. "I took off for the scrub. I ran like hell for a long time. They didn't get me because they didn't know where I went to. By that night, I was miles and miles away." He puffed proudly his cigarette.

"Where did you go to, Jack? You would have been in strife if you had have been caught, wouldn't you?"

He opened his eyes wide and rolled them in an exaggeration of hopelessness.

"Aw, I would have been buggered," he admitted, relaxing his shoulders to a limp position. "They'd have flogged shit out of me. Nah, I couldn't let them catch me. I pissed off back to the Albert River. There was a mob there. They used to come and go all the time but there was usually about seven or eight there."

Jack was puffing heavily, as if he had physically relived his quick dash back to the Albert River. I sat watching him for a while as his cheeks blew in and out.

"Jack," I asked, after a while. "What about your father; what did he do for a living?"

He looked at me in a manner which indicated that I should have known the answer.

"He worked on a station," he said, in a matter-of-fact way. "Nearly every blackfella worked on stations. They were the best at it. Poor old bugger."

As he spoke these words, he dropped his chin onto his chest. He stayed thus for a few moments and I didn't disturb him. I waited for him to continue his account of his father.

"Yes," he said, at last. "Poor old bugger got it rough, all right. They all did, for that matter." He stopped again, collecting his thoughts. Suddenly, he shook his head vigorously.

"You know, he was tied to a tree once and flogged with a stockwhip. Another time he was hit on the shin with a crowbar. It smashed his bone. Broke his leg clean through."

The rapidity of his speech surprised me. He became upset. I rose from my seat and placed a hand upon him. He looked at me pitifully, with a look that I would have thought an old man like Cyclone Jack was incapable of. He shrugged his shoulders at my action.

"Ah, well, Bill," he said. "It's gone now. It's all in the past. He's dead now. Been dead for a long time. He died at a place called Duchess. That's not really a long way from here." He lifted an arm and pointed a finger in the direction of the main road. "I haven't been there for years," he explained.

I wondered if it would be unkind to allow Jack to bring back memories by allowing him to continue his narrative about his father. Perhaps I should alter the course of our discussion. Or, perhaps I should go and leave the now-pensive old man to his memories. He solved the dilemma for me as he threw his hands in the air.

"Ah, bugger," he exclaimed. "It's all gone. Anyway, I want to tell you a few things about it. My father, I mean."

"Ah, Jack," I said, comfortingly. "Why bring back bad and bitter memories? Why not let sleeping dogs lie?" I regained my seat and carelessly tossed a smoke onto the table in front of him as a sign that the current conversation was at an end.

"My father saw a lot of bad things," he persisted. "A lot happened to him, too." I held up a hand in order to stop him from further conversation.

"Jack," I said to him. "I don't want you upsetting yourself over things that happened long ago. Now, I know you want to tell me things that happened in the old days but, if you'd rather not, we could easily talk about something else."

He smiled condescendingly at my remarks as he shook his head slowly. "I won't get upset, Bill," he assured me. "I get a bit carried away sometimes, that's all."

"Well, I would like to know of any other mistreatments he may have suffered." I held up a warning finger. "No bullshit now though." We looked at each other sternly for a few moments; Jack appeared slightly hurt at my proviso.

"I wouldn't tell you any bullshit," he frowned. "No need for that." I realised that I had said a stupid thing. Of course, why would old Jack want to tell me lies? He, like most people, might exaggerate a little at times, but that would be his limit.

He tugged at his ear as he cast his memory back.

"He told me that some other tribe were having corroboree once and these blacktrackers rode up and started shooting them. When they got close enough they cut 'em up with swords. They just shot 'em. But the officer — he was a white fella — he had a big sword. The bastard!"[44]

"That's a bit crude," I remarked. "Where did this happen?"

"Near the Logan, I think," he answered. "I'm not sure. He told me my grandfather used to live there with the tribe, you know."

I paused momentarily in my note-taking, trying to visualise the scene of the painted and dancing Aborigines as they dropped in their tracks.

"Another thing he told me about was how the troopers used to raid the camps and piss off with the young gins. If the tribe kicked up a fuss they would get shot. But the tribe get payback one way or another. 'Course, it wasn't only the blacktrackers what used to pinch the young gins. A lot of those white fellas came at that caper, too. From what my father told me, most of them station fellas rode down the young gins. You can guess why. The big trouble was, when the blackfellas went to get their gins back, they got shot or they sooled the dogs onto them." Jack sighed and held his hand up to his head several times during our conversation. He now placed his head between his hands and squeezed.

"What's the matter?" I asked him.

"Aw, got a bit of a headache," he replied, lowering his head closer to the ground. "Don't get many."

"Too much smoking," I chided. "Or too much of that shitty tea you drink."

He smiled slightly and and got to his feet and groaned. "Hummm," he agreed. "It might be. I think I'll have a bit of a lie down."

"Might be a good idea, mate. Give your brain a rest." He looked at me with a stare which suggested that I should go and do the impossible! He moved over to his mattress and slowly settled himself down. I rose and walked toward the door.

"See you later, Jack," I told him, and left him to rest.

Although Jack had related some horrible stories to me, there are many other accounts of man's inhumanity to man which are well documented. One of the best known, for instance, is the Myall Creek massacre. On the run was camped a tribe of natives, some fifty strong, who were on friendly terms with the station hands. There is no reason to believe that they were otherwise than inoffensive. However, during the absence of the manager, Mr Hobbs, a stockkeeper named Kilmeister and seven others made a descent upon the blacks for the purpose of "clearing them out". It was an unapproved attack, actuated simply by motives of brutality, although an attempt was afterwards made to excuse it on the score that the tribe had been spearing cattle. The unfortunate natives — men, women and children — were roped together, and some of them further secured by handcuffs. Then they were driven out some distance, to be slaughtered in cold blood, like sheep. The manager returned to the station a few days later and noticed the absence of the blacks. He gained an inkling of what had transpired, and paid a visit to a distant part of the run. A horrifying spectacle confronted him. On the ground were the remains of at least thirty natives, the bodies mangled and half-burnt. Some were those of children. He discovered in the course of his investigation that swords had been used by the butchers as well as pistols and that the blacks had no chance of fighting for their lives. (A large number of the victims had been decapitated and horribly mutilated.) A station hand told a straightforward tale of how the party of stockmen had carried away the blacks, of how he had heard the reports of firearms, and how the men had returned with blood-stained swords.[45]

Other massacres, well documented by historians, occurred at Condamine, Long Lagoon (near Ingham) and Pine River. At Condamine, the blacks were found holding a corroboree with the rest of their tribe. The troopers, surrounding them, fired volley after volley into the crowd of painted, dancing figures, for whom there was no escape. Then, armed with swords, they leapt in to finish the work at close quarters.[46]

An alternative means of destruction was employed by the owner of Long Lagoon. Rations powerfully laced with strychnine were made available to the blacks. The following morning more than a hundred corpses were stretched out. There were no survivors.[47]

The mass murder which occurred at Pine River (just north of Brisbane), like the others, was completely unnecessary. Blacks in this area were quite friendly and, in fact, willing to assist whites, for instance by minding cattle or cutting bark. However, unknown numbers perished as a result of a feast of "death pudding". Author Edgar Foreman states that, "As a boy, I rode through a small pocket of what was known as Rush Creek and saw scores of bleached bones including a complete skeleton. Also, at Whitesides Station, the 'pudding' was responsible for the death of 'fifty or sixty'."[48]

Kilcoy, in south-eastern Queensland, also witnessed the death scene of countless blacks who had consumed the evil "death pudding", the macabre name given to this damper of flour and poison. In one incident, shepherds had placed enough of the poisoned flour in a hut to kill some sixty blacks who subsequently died in abject agony.[49]

Atrocities too numerous to mention were perpetrated by white upon black. It was, for instance, considered "manly" to own a tobacco stopper (cork) or a pipe rammer made from the dried and cured finger of a blackfellow. How the owner obtained the grizzly digit would be better imagined than described.[50]

In *The Trooper Police of Australia*, A.L. Haydon recounts a further variation of the atrocities committed during this period of Australian history.

A stockman, infatuated by a young black woman, severed her husband's head and forced the protesting gin to wear the gruesome thing around her neck.[51] George Carrington writes:

> I have seen two large pits, covered with branches and brush, and secured by a few stones, and the pits themselves were full of dead blackfellows, of all ages and both sexes. On another occasion, I was travelling on a road where, for more than a quarter of a mile, the air was tainted with the putrefaction of corpses, which lay along the ridges, just as they had fallen.[52]

In another incident an eyewitness recounts:

A bullock had been slaughtered by station hands when one of the hands, a lowly character indeed, threw the bleeding guts with a slap around the naked breast of a young, inoffending black woman. The lubra smiled bashfully, not being familiar with the white man's sense of humour and not realising just what a disgusting insult and degrading act had befallen her.[53]

Camp-fire yarns frequently consisted of such malicious brags as "The only good nigger is a dead nigger" and "I now shoot on sight, killed to date, 37".[54]

But enough! Enough of this white man's legacy! And yet these statements and actions were no doubt made by men who believed they were pursuing fine principles and fair play!

If my words sound brusque and derisive, I am sorry, but it is my theory that if the white man had left his fly buttoned up, it is probable that the hostilities between white man and black in the early, turbulent years, would have been avoided. Of course, white exploitation and dishonesty played their part in bringing about black uprising. And yet it was not always the case that a state of hostility existed between black and white. In the very beginning, black subservience to the white gentry ensured that relations would be harmonious. It was not until the white employers cheated on their black employees that rejection of white society began in earnest (tribal violations excluded, of course). Nevertheless, many station owners respected their black assistants to the extent that, if danger threatened, they conscientiously protected them from harm. Why not? It was cheap labour.

In the biography of Tom Petrie, published in 1904, his daughter Constance writes of the blacks at North Pine, twenty-five kilometres from Brisbane:

When my father employed the blacks, they were always kind and considerate about him. They are naturally an affectionate

> people, and he with his good and kindly disposition, and his fun — for the blacks so enjoy a joke — was very popular with them all. Nowadays it is seldom one sees an aboriginal, but some years ago, when they would come at times and camp round here, it was amusing to see the excitement when they found their old friend in the mood for a yarn . . . A good-natured people they surely are, for amusement at their expense does not call forth resentment; rather they would join in the laugh. On first coming, nearly forty-five years ago, to North Pine, which is sixteen miles by road from Brisbane, the country round about was wild bush . . . The blacks were very good and helpful, lending a hand to split and fence and put up stockyards, and they would help look after the cattle and yard them at night. For the young fellow was all alone, no white man would come near him, being in dread of the blacks. Here he was among two hundred of them, and came to no harm. With their help he had got a yard made, and a hut erected, he obtained flour, tea, sugar, and tobacco from Brisbane, and leaving these rations in the hut, in charge of an old aboriginal, went away again to Brisbane, and was away this time for a fortnight. Fifty head of cattle he also left in charge of two young blacks, trusting them to yard these at night, etc; and to enable the young darkies to do this, he allowed them each the use of a horse and saddle. On his return all was as it should be, not even a bit of tobacco missing! And those who know no better say the aborigines are treacherous and untrustworthy! Father says he could always trust them; and his experience has been that if you treated them kindly they would do anything for you.[55]

Tom Petrie, who more or less grew up with Aborigines, knew more about them perhaps than any white man of the day. He expounded that it was the broken promises and the deception which caused the blacks to distrust the white man. Tom Petrie's experiences with blacks were unique. He arrived in Australia in 1831 and the family moved to Brisbane in 1837, where his father took up the position of Superintendent of Works. The family home was built on a stretch of land which is now the corner of Queen and Wharf Streets. The surrounding area, where

Aborigines camped, was still thick scrub. As there were very few white children with whom to play, young Tom spent most of his time with the black children. He learned to speak their language quite fluently and grew up as a great and trusted friend. Even so, Petrie had deep respect for the customs of the Aborigines and recognised that, accommodated within the custom structure, was both the need and the desire to fight. The need was to stop interlopers from encroaching upon tribal land and the desire exists because, like the white man, Aborigines *wanted* to fight. During the 1800s, the largest and most popular fighting ground was the area which is known as the Brisbane Exhibition Ground.

Petrie's daughter, Constance, told in his biography of many experiences her father had with blacks.

> One young fellow, learning to ride in those days, was thrown several times. My father, vexed with the mare ridden, mounted her himself, and giving the animal a sharp cut with his riding whip, sent her off at full gallop. He carried a revolver in his belt, which he always had handy, as often the blacks would get him to shoot kangaroos they had surrounded and hunted into a waterhole. The mare galloped on, then, stopping suddenly, somehow threw her rider in spite of his good seat. The first thing he remembered afterwards was seeing a company of blacks collected around him, crying, and one old man was on his knees sucking his back, where the hammer of the revolver had struck. They then carried him to his hut, and in the morning he was nothing but stiff after his adventure.
>
> And there was no white man about! To him they were always kind and thoughtful . . . They resented unkindness. For instance, the owner of a station some distance away used to have his cattle speared and killed. Father would remonstrate (with the Aborigines) and ask why, and the blacks would answer: It was because if that man caught any of them, he would shoot them down like dogs! Then they told this tale: A number of blacks were on the man's run, scattered here and there, looking for wild honey and possums, when the owner

came upon them and shooting one young fellow, first broke his leg, then another shot in the head killed him. The superior white man then hid himself to watch what would happen. Presently the father came looking for his son, and he was shot; the mother coming after met the same fate. My father knew the blacks well who told him this, and was satisfied they spoke truthfully. It may strike the reader why he did not make use of his information and bring punishment to the offender? Well, because in those days a blackfellow's evidence counted as nothing, and no good would therefore be gained, but rather the opposite, as bitterness would be increased, and the blacks get the worst of it.[56]

Tom Petrie also had cause to dislike the behaviour of the Native Mounted Police. On one particular occasion a neighbouring squatter claimed (wrongfully) that blacks had speared some of his cattle and so he sent to Police Headquarters at Sandgate for assistance. It was later established that one of the squatter's employees, who was afraid of the blacks, rode to Sandgate where he made this false accusation.

Unfortunately, Cyclone Jack's nemesis, Lieutenant Frederick Wheeler, with his detachment, was detailed to attend to the matter. Of course, he dispersed the blacks with alacrity. Constance Petrie writes:

While out riding in the bush, my father heard a great row, and a voice calling, "Round them up, boys!" And on galloping up he came upon a number of poor blacks — men, women and children — all in a mob like so many wild cattle, surrounded by mounted black police. The poor creatures tried to run to their friend for protection, and he enquired of the officer in charge what was the meaning of it all. The officer — a white man, and one, by the way, who was noted for his inhuman cruelty — replied that they merely wished to see who was who. But my father knew that if he hadn't turned up, a number of the poor things would have been shot. Can any wonder there were murders committed by the blacks, seeing how they were sometimes treated? This same police officer (Wheeler, by name) later on was to have been hanged for whipping a poor creature to death, but he escaped and fled from the country. It is possible he is still alive. His victim was a young blackfellow, whom he had tied to a verandah post, and then brutally flogged till he died.[57]

(Wheeler may have fled the country but Cyclone Jack claimed he had been caught by the blacks who then carried out "payback".)

The story continues, as Tom Petrie remonstrated with the squatter: "You're a nice sort of fellow; how could you cause those poor blacks to be shot like that? You know perfectly well they did not kill your cattle."[58] The squatter excused himself from blame by claiming that he had no knowledge of the affair.

This then was the way of life inflicted upon blacks in the early days. In finality, it is worth reiterating that, if promises had been honoured, Aboriginal laws and customs respected — after first taking the time to understand them — and if Aboriginal women had not been exploited and violated, the outcome for Queensland could have been . . . nay . . . would have been totally different. Such is the value of hindsight!

But, unfortunately, black-white relations quickly deteriorated into the terrible scourge that was to endure for over two hundred years!

"Gib me dat tin-opener"

The sun had swung low over the Georgina River, causing the long, thin shadows of the paperbark trees to fall onto the dry, dusty Mitchell grass. I gazed over to Cyclone Jack's rusty tin shed and saw wisps of smoke worming their way from beneath the iron roof. The wind had dropped and the chill air began to settle. I decided not to visit him again that day as he would be busily preparing his evening tucker. The fact that I would be forced to stay another night in order to speak further with him the following day did not concern me because I rather enjoyed this isolated little town. It occurred to me that I had better locate Ruby and ask her if she could find a shake-down for another night. I looked over to the huge windmill and saw her sitting on the built-up bank of the turkey nest,[59] talking with a mob of Aborigines who seemed to be agitated about something. When I walked across to them I soon discovered the cause of their excitement. Lying beside the water trough were two large goannas. Ruby explained to me that they had come down to the cattle trough to drink. The way Ruby told it, I doubt if the goannas had had a chance to get their tongues wet before some well-aimed stones flattened them.

"Plenty tucker now," one of the group said to me.

"The shop can keep its camp pie." We all laughed at the young man's impudent remark. I picked one goanna up by the tail and it was indeed a monster. I had to use both arms to clear it from the ground. Even so, its head lolled on the dirt, the tongue hanging limply.

In no time at all, the group had a fire going and the night's meal was carelessly tossed on to the blazing logs. The amount of meat on a goanna is quite surprising and, if it can be cooked without being burnt, it tastes rather like oily tuna. The reptile, more or less, cooks in its own oil, of which it has a prodigious amount.

I slept cold, huddled up in the cabin of my Datsun. I envied Ruby a little. She was cuddled up in a large piece of hessian and was lying between two fires which the group had built. At first light I went over to Jack's place. Smoke was already issuing from his hut and the flames of his fire threw his moving shadow outside, taking on the appearance of some ghostly spectre. He heard me coming and, on noticing my shiver, he shook his head with disgust.

"You mad, you bugger," he said. "Plenty bloody room here. You could have camped on those bags there." I looked in the corner to where the bags were stacked and realised that if I had passed the night there, I would have shared the shake-down with at least forty million fleas, ants, spiders and all those other things that crawl around in the night. Not all the insect repellent in the world — not even Jack's kerosene rag — would have kept the hordes at bay.

"As a matter of fact, Jack, I was going to sleep here but there was a program on the car radio I wanted to listen to." It was a harmless lie, an expedient untruth. The billy was balanced on the rocks over the fire and I looked forward to a cup of steaming coffee. A cup of anything. Even Jack's ghastly bottlebrush concoction would, at least, alter the taste in my mouth.

The billy boiled fairly quickly and, to my relief, Jack left enough water in the billy to enable me to make a reasonable mug of coffee. We sat in front of the fire, each savouring the delights of that early morning cuppa.

"I feel a bit sore in the chest this morning," Jack complained. He put his hand beneath his dustcoat and gently massaged his chest. He looked a bit grey in appearance I remarked on this.

"Aw," he shrugged. "Must be a bit of bone trouble. It comes and goes."

"How do you feel, Jack? Do you feel like talking or do you want me to bugger off?"

"I'm not that bloody crook," he replied. "No, no, you stay. It'll be gone soon. Soon as it warms up a bit, it'll go away. It always does."

I nodded my agreement at his forecast. I hoped that the cold wind didn't spring up again.

"Why? You want to talk some more?" he asked.

"Only if you're up to it, Jack," I replied. "There are a few things I'd like to ask you about; for instance, have you ever heard of Tom Petrie?"

He cast his eyes down, thinking deeply.

"Can't say I have," he admitted. "Yet the name rung around in my head. Who is he?"

"He's a bloke who lived around Brisbane about the time I reckon your grandfather was alive," I told him. "He was a good bloke with Aborigines. I just thought you might have heard the name."

"No, I don't know him," he added, after thinking a little longer. "He'd be dead now though, wouldn't he?"

"Dead and rotted," I replied, insensitively.

He dismissed the subject and removed a crumpled piece of paper from his pocket. He flattened it out on the table and peered closely at it. Suddenly, he stabbed at it with his finger.

"Yesssss," he drew out the word. "This mongrel, 'ere."

I waited patiently for him to continue.

"A lot of talk about this one," he said. "Long ago."

I held out my hand to receive the piece of paper. On it was written the word, "Bly". It meant absolutely nothing to me. I waited for Jack to explain but he remained silent.

"Well," I asked. "What is it? What does it mean?"

Jack was sitting on the very edge of his box. Clearly, he was perturbed.

"He was one of them," he told me. "He was one of those white fellas that ordered the blacktrackers around."

"Do you mean he was a policeman?"

"I think so," he replied. "I heard my father talk about him. He told me he was a bad bastard. That's all I can remember."

"Well, don't worry, Jack. I'll see what I can find out about him when I get back to Brisbane. I'll let you know what I find out."

"You coming back up here again?" He seemed surprised.

"Yes," I informed him. "I'll be back."

I made some notes in my book and folded Jack's piece of paper inside it. He rose from his box and wandered outside. The sun was fully up and, thankfully, there was no wind. I followed him out and offered him a cigarette which I had lit for him. He took it and slowly sat down on the ground, facing the sun.

"Soon makes you warm, eh," he remarked, rubbing

his chest again. "When it gets on my bones, the pain goes away a bit."

"Give us a look," I said, my hand already undoing the untidy knot which held his dustcoat together.

"I can't see anything," he said, assisting me with his coat. I bared his chest and was astounded to find how bony he really was. There was not a scrap of flesh on him! I tapped his sternum and ribs with an inexperienced finger, hearing the dull thud it produced.

"You've got arthritis," I guessed. "That's the same thing Ruby has except hers is in her knee." He looked at me as if I were the Flying Doctor. Such admiration.

"It's nearly gone," he said. "See, I told you the sun would fix it. Does it every time."

"Good," I answered. "Do you really feel well enough to talk some more?"

"Aw, I'll talk till the cows come home," he responded.

"Well," I began. "I have heard and read that blackfellows ate each other." I stopped short, realising how indelicately I had broached the subject. Old Jack looked at me in amazement, his lips disappearing into his mouth.

"What a lot of bullshit they talk about. Christ! I've never seen a blackfella *that* hungry."

Although the subject was a gruesome one, I found it difficult not to smile at the answer Jack had given.

"It has been written that, in certain parts of Queensland, young girls have more or less been given up as a sacrifice. They reckon old men were eaten, too."

"Well, that's the best I've heard for a long time," he said, clicking his tongue. "Even in the old times — you know, in the tribes — the only blackfellas that were eaten were the clever old fellas, or real good fighters.

They only ate little bits of them, you know. They believed that, if they ate a bit of a clever blackfella, they would be clever too." He paused for a moment. "Christ! They didn't eat 'em like a bit of bloody 'roo meat!"

He shifted from one fleshless buttock to the other on the unyielding ground.

"Sometimes," he resumed his explanation, "sometimes if a great fighter got killed in a fight, some of the tribe might eat a bit of him so they would be good fighters like him. It was the custom in those days, you know, the old days. It was what they believed."

I was not prepared to continue with this line of conversation. Jack was slightly upset and I was not going to exacerbate the situation.

"You blokes must have had a great time when the bunya nuts were ripe," I offered, hoping to erase the previous subject from his mind. He certainly took the bait.

"Aw, yes," he replied, eyes beaming and smiling widely. "Aw, great time. That's the best time I can remember. Dance. All dance there. Aw, lot of people. Come from everywhere." He waved his arms slowly in a circle to emphasise his words. "But it didn't take long for those white fellas to bugger it up." His smile had changed to a scowl.

"How, Jack?" I enquired. "How did they bugger it up?"

"Ah, well," he answered. "They cut 'em down. Cut down all the bloody trees." He made descriptive movements with his arms again. "My father had lot of fight over his tree," he said. "They cut it down in front of him."

"Owned a tree?" I queried. "How did he manage that?"

"They all owned trees," he informed me. "See, if a blackfella owned a tree, the other blackfellas could not eat the nuts off that tree unless he said so. I remember there was big corroboree that time. There used to be t'ousands there. They come from everywhere; miles away. There used to be miles of camps . . . all along."

"And you remember all that, do you, Jack?"

"Yes, I know all that." He gave a half-laugh. "By gee," he mused. "There was a lot of fight, too."

"How come, Jack?" I asked. "What did they fight about?"

"Aw, well," he explained. "There were a lot of tribes here. All different, you know. Different ways; different talk; different women." He leered sideways at me. Had he been a younger man, that look would have had lust written all over it! We both smiled. He was puffing a little and he began to rub his chest again and I wondered if he had a complaint other than arthritis.

"You'd better have a bit of a rest, Jack," I advised him. "I want to go over to the mill and see Ruby. I'll call back later."

"Yes," he agreed. "I feel like a bit of a rest." He lay down and turned onto his side, trying to settle his hip into the hard earth. He pulled a clod across and used it for a pillow.

"You right now?" I asked. "I'll see you later."

He nodded his head in acknowledgment and I turned to walk across the dry, dusty paddock towards the windmill.

I was about half way across when the mob that had befriended Ruby began to wave and yell to me. I changed direction and headed for the group. Ruby was with them and I singled her out and asked her what all the drama was abut. Before she could reply, the young person to whom I had given the tin-opener pushed his way through to the front of the group.

"Hey," he uttered, somewhat insolently. "Gib me dat tin-opener you got."

"I gave you one yesterday. What have you done with it?"

"I bin lose dat one. You gib me, eh?" He was quite amused by the fact that he had lost the opener I had given him. His cheekiness was encouraged by the giggles of some of the younger girls.

"No, mate," I replied. "I haven't got one to spare. You had better go and look for the one I gave you."

The smile cleared from his face and it appeared that he was going to get nasty. He curled his lips and scowled.

"Hey, look out," he said, menacingly. "You better gib me dat," he made a fist. "I'll smash ya."

I smiled broadly at him, which did nothing for his ego.

"Now listen, Bunji[60]," I replied, moving closer to him. "You don't want to talk like that. You just might happen to get a clip in the ear. How would you like a sore binna?"[61]

He was taken aback by my crisp yet friendly retaliation. His vanity weakened as he hung his head slightly. It hurt me to see the pride, albeit misplaced, ebb from him. That was not what I wanted to do to him. I reached out my arm and grabbed him lightly on his bicep.

"Hey," I said, soothingly. "Come on. Come over to the truck and I'll open your tin for you." The giggling had stopped and we began to walk over to the Datsun.

"Don't tell me you're still hungry after that bloody great feed of goanna," I said, jokingly. "You'll get fat like some of those white f'la."

His dignity had now returned and he laughed out loud. We were all happy again. As it happened, he had no tin to open and his bravado of the five minutes or so before purely an act to impress the younger members of the mob. Just as I thought. We became quite friendly after that brief confrontation. He was of small build, bum fluff becoming obvious on his chin. His only dress was a pair of frayed denim shorts which were far too small for him. As he walked away, it was quite humorous to watch his skinny little arse moving up and down with each step. He told me he had spent most of his life around the Georgina River and lived largely off the land. He had gone to Mt Isa some years ago but the number of white people and the noise had frightened him and he returned to the Georgina. He occasionally came into Urandangie "for woman".

I turned my attention to Ruby, who had remained silent during the last few minutes.

"How did you sleep last night, Ruby?" I enquired.

"Like a log," she replied. "I was so tired out from walking all over the place. How about you?"

"I nearly froze," I replied. "I spent the night on the front seat of the Datsun."

"You should have come over to where we were. We had the biggest fire."

"Where were you?"

"We started out near the mill and ended up on the dry river bed," she huggled her shoulders, suggesting comfort. "The sand was nice and warm."

I could have kicked myself! Why didn't I think of that? The great Georgina River was as dry as a bone and the sand soaked up the sun during the day and it remained warm practically all night. "Some bushman!" I chided myself. Ruby noticed my chagrin.

"We looked for you but we couldn't see you," one of

the group said. And no wonder. I had nosed the Datsun under some low-hanging branches of a tree, and I would have been hidden from view.

"Feel like some tea?" Ruby asked. "We've still got the fire going down there and the water'll be boiling."

"Can't think of anything better," I accepted. "You got real tea?" I asked, cautiously. I was not risking that bottlebrush stuff again.

"Yes," Ruby looked at me in an odd way. "Bushells."

We all went down to where the fire was blazing and, sure enough, the water was boiling away fitfully. One of the young girls quickly made some tea and we sat on the sand, yarning away for about two hours.

Having gathered enough research material to keep me out of mischief for about two months, I decided it was time I made tracks for home. I mentioned my plans to Ruby, in case she had made some particular arrangements which would keep her in Urandangie.

"No," she said, eagerly. "I've got no reason to stay here any longer. It'll be good to get 'ome."

I returned to the Datsun and began loading up. We jumped in and, after saying goodbye to Jack and the others, headed off in a swirl of dust on the way to Dajarra. Soon we were thrashing out way back over that stretch of terrible road to the Mt Isa turn-off. When we reached the bitumen I stopped and we both shook ourselves thoroughly to try to rid ourselves of the bulldust. Ruby reckoned the road had so many turns in it that it would break a snake's back.

We arrived in Dajarra and, after drinking the best cup of tea I had tasted since we left, Ruby removed her camp oven and the rest of "me campin' gear" from the ute.

"You comin' back?" she enquired.

"I'm coming back," I answered. "But it won't be for a while. I have a lot of work to do."

"Work?" she looked puzzled. "What sort of work?"

"Well, reading, mostly," I replied. "And chewing headache tablets."

She did not respond to my facetiousness. After a brief goodbye — in Ruby's customary manner — I belted my faithful old Datsun into gear and continued on the long drag back to Brisbane.

"He shot him through the head"

After a few days back in the city, eating good meals again, and after having thoroughly scrubbed the Urandangie dust from my hair, I sat and contemplated the last few weeks. Foremost in my mind, of course, was old Cyclone Jack. My first move, therefore, was to visit the State Archives and try to track down some of the astonishing claims he had made as we sat in that rusty tin and bag hut up in the bush. As I patiently untied the neatly bound records, the name "Bligh" sprang from the pages. The name Cyclone Jack had given me was "Bly", but after reading through some of the material, I realised there could be no doubt that Jack had spelled the name incorrectly.

Lieutenant John O'Connell Bligh emerged from those dusty old archival records as a heartless fiend, much in the same mould as the infamous Lieutenant Frederick Wheeler. Bligh was the grandson of Captain Bligh of *Bounty* fame. On 7 April 1853, he was appointed Sublieutenant in the Native Mounted Police Force, and quickly made a name for himself as a zealous officer.[62] Not long after he was commissioned into the force he tracked and captured the escaped convict, John Fahay. He found Fahay living with blacks at the head of the Mary River, officially reporting the success of his capture on 20 December 1854.

Bligh was transferred to the Maryborough district and on 1 June 1857 was promoted to the rank of First Lieutenant. On 8 July 1861 he was appointed Acting Commandant (later, Commandant) of the Native Mounted Police. Although he had moved up the ranks to the most senior position in only eight years, Bligh had some anxious moments during that period of service. He had battled flooded creeks, been caught out in the wet with bogged horses and, at one stage, was assaulted by two troopers, Corporal Donald and Trooper Dick. Bligh had ordered Trooper Dick to do sentry duty but Dick refused and knocked Bligh to the ground, threatening to handcuff him. Corporal Donald entered the fray with a nulla-nulla. The two troopers were under the command of Lieutenant Frederick Walker, who had told the two troopers not to take any nonsense from Bligh. If Bligh were to "bounce" them, they were to bounce him back.[63]

During his tours of duty in the Dawson, Wide Bay and Burnett districts, Bligh enjoyed the reputation of being a zealous and conscientious officer. His superior, Lieutenant John Murray, expressed the view that Bligh was "a good officer" (although Murray himself was dismissed from the Force in 1861 for improper conduct and "general unfitness for his duties", the reason being given elsewhere in this book). On 2 May 1857, Bligh was appointed Commandant for the Wide Bay district and two days later he was recommended for the post of Magistrate by the Commandant of the Native Police Force, Edric Morisset. Previous to this he had been appointed a Justice of the Peace.

There can be no doubt that the township of Maryborough had problems with rebellious Aborigines but it is most likely that the troubles were brought about largely through white ill-treatment of blacks in the first instance. However, for whatever reason, on the morning of 3 February 1860, Maryborough erupted into violence.

Perhaps the scene had been set during the last week of January. Bligh entertained a party of friends at his Cooper's Plains (Maryborough) camp. Among the guests were the storekeeper, a squatter and Lieutenant Charles Phibbs. The camp sergeant, Sergeant Gasson, was absent. During the course of the party, "indecent liberties" were taken with Gasson's wife by Bligh, Phibbs and others. On his return to camp, Gasson heard of this and immediately removed his wife from the camp for her own protection and informed the offenders that he intended to report the "disgraceful affair" to Commandant Morisset. Several days later, Bligh rode into Maryborough and publicly dismissed Gasson from the Force for alleged drunkenness. Gasson felt grossly humiliated and therefore wasted no time in revealing to the townspeople just what a cur this fellow Bligh really was.

The revelations were accompanied by escalating rumour and gossip. Certainly Bligh's reputation was not one becoming an officer and a magistrate. The rumours reached the Government Resident, Arthur Halloran, and, on the evening of 2 February, he paid Bligh a visit at his barracks to discuss the affair. Halloran was obviously not amused at the scandal nor by the dismissal of Sergeant Gasson. Several weeks later Halloran, who was also Commissioner for Crown Lands, reinstated Gasson as his orderly and footed the bill for a horse and saddle for him, an action to which Bligh took singular exception.

It was during the early hours of the morning following Bligh's confrontation with Halloran that the drama began. Bligh and his native troopers galloped into the township and attacked a group of blacks who were camping quietly and harmlessly near a store. One was shot dead and the rest were chased into the river. Another group of blacks camped nearby received similar treatment. One old black, known as "Snatchem", who was a permanent resident in the town and had the reputation of being a good worker, became exhausted and pleaded with Bligh for mercy but, within view of men, women and children, Bligh shot the old man in the back. Bligh then captured another old man who was also a resident in the town, handcuffed him and marched him away to be shot. The remainder of the blacks tried to escape into the river, but Bligh, intent on murder, procured a boat and, standing in the bow, shot another flailing, exhausted blackfellow through the head.

Opinion on this cold-blooded act was divided among the citizens of Maryborough. A number of the people applauded the action and subscribed to a fund which enabled the citizens to buy and present Bligh with a sword — "of which the blade is 3 feet in length and handsomely decorated with embroidered flowers and other devices".

An advertisement in the *Wide Bay Chronicle* on 28 February 1861 reads:

> The public are respectfully informed the sword subscribed for by the inhabitants of Maryborough to be presented to Lieutenant Bligh, of the Native Mounted Police, "for his services in suppressing the outrages of the blacks", is now on view at the Maryborough Inn for a short time.[64]

The advertisement was signed "Geo. Howard". It was intended that the sword be presented to Bligh as a token of esteem for his services. The sword "with a sheath is enclosed in a very neat case altogether forming a very handsome present". Well that sword, and the manner in which John O'Connell Bligh, JP, "earned" it, created a furore in the small township of Maryborough. Many people who had witnessed the killing of the blacks were quite convinced that Bligh was in a drunken state. It was considered in many quarters that the black troopers were drunk also. A letter to the editor of the *Moreton Bay Courier* of 2 March 1861 observed that ". . . troopers are taught to drink spirits I have no doubt, and very soon they become fond of it. There is a law, I believe, yet in force, to punish those who supply an aboriginal with spirits, but possibly the officers may feel some compunction in doing so, when they, themselves (I mean only some of them), set the example of such continual intemperance." The letter was signed, "One who has seen too much of the Native Police."

In view of the past record of good, reliable (albeit murderous!) service and the experience gained during his years as an officer, it can be safely assumed that he was, indeed, under the influence of liquor. There can be no doubt, either, that the majority of people — not only in the town of Maryborough, but throughout Queensland — believed that the Native Mounted Police, led by their white officers, were bloodthirsty and merciless killers. Oddly, many squatters (for whose protection the force was established in the first instance) held the Native Police in contempt and spoke of them in most disparaging terms!

A typical "Letter to the Editor" states:

> Sir, it is impossible for you, or any of your correspondents, to say too much about this mismanaged and most disgraceful force, and nothing but the grossest of cowardice, or most culpable blindness to all facts, leads people now to argue in its

favour. This very town has witnessed scenes in its neighbourhood which one hardly dare relate — the bloodiest of murders committed upon the innocent natives at one time, followed by the greatest solicitude upon the part of those who saw the deeds that they should not be talked about. It has witnessed a drunken officer, too beastly almost to sit upon a horse, ride forth with the avowed and inflamed intention of "shooting down the wretches", and in a very few hours afterwards its inhabitants have been busy again in shielding the miscreant from his proper doom.

The force should be done away with at once. Every father, mother, sister, and brother in Queensland should join in the holy cry. It is fast demoralizing the whole community, and turning Christians into the abject and wicked apologists of men, whose trade is to take life, and yet cannot do so without perpetrating murder. The very notion that these "Gracemere Pets" — these inferior creatures — are suitable to defend the lives of Englishmen is revolting, and craven must a people be who crave for them . . .

I am, Sir,
A Squatter.[65]

Strong words from one of those whom the Native Mounted Police were employed to protect!

Many squatters who, in fact, had employed Aborigines on their stations for many years, on learning of an impending visit from the Native Police — the troopers — concealed and protected those Aborigines in the sure knowledge that, if they were seen, they would be "dispersed", and such dispersal invariably meant shooting them. Probably the most devastating letter which was written to an editor regarding the Bligh affair was published in the *Moreton Bay Courier*. It was given the heading "Lieutenant Bligh's sword".

Sir, — Through the medium of the press of New South Wales and Queensland, the public have been duly informed that "the inhabitants of Maryborough" have purchased the highest reward of courage, the emblem of bravery — a sword — to present to John O'Connell Bligh, Esq., for certain meritorious actions said to be performed by him on the 3rd February, 1860; but as the said public is not aware of the precise nature of this "very meritorious conduct", or of the gallant heroism which called forth such a noble reward — a reward hitherto only bestowed upon the "bravest of the brave" — permit me, Mr. Editor, to state, for general information, the circumstances under which the said sword has been purchased . . .

On the morning of the 3rd February, there commenced a change, apparently, in the tactics or habits of the officers, for Mr Bligh, with a party of police, rode into town early, and lest, apparently, the change should not be noticed, fired several shots at a few blacks encamped near Cleary's; then came into East Maryborough, charged a camp near Mr Melville's, drove the poor creatures from it — some through the town, some into the river — and commenced butchering them forthwith. "Darkey", who had been constantly employed in the town — who could have been apprehended at any moment, had there been any desire, or occasion, was shot down opposite Mr Palmer's, where his body was left, and subsequently roasted. "Young Snatchem", an excellent and industrious black, was driven into the river, near the public wharf — scores of men, women and children stood by, and Lieut. John O'Connell Bligh stationed himself in the bow of a boat, which was in readiness, and forty or fifty shots were actually fired, five or six by Mr. Bligh himself. The boat overtook him (the black) in an exhausted state, and the "gallant hero" — the deserver of a sword — lowered his carbine, and shot the defenceless, tired, unresisting wretch in the back. "Yankine", who was then wounded, has since recovered. Against him, there never was a single charge. Another poor fellow, blind in one eye, an old grey headed man, was taken prisoner, triumphantly marched in handcuffs through the town, led out some miles by these bloodthirsty brutes, and has never SINCE been seen. The blacks immediately brought in word that he had been shot near the Six-Mile Creek, and as the old creature was well known here, and a frequent visitor at certain houses, it is beyond doubt that he too had been, if possible, more barbarously murdered than the others . . . A people who could submit to see their benighted, confiding fellows thus slaughtered — see those they had employed, and in employing, had offered HOSPITALITY, and pledged their SINCERITY to — butchered, were capable of sinking even deeper, and DEEPER they sank.

> On the following Monday a meeting was convened, a chairman WAS procured for it, and resolutions were actually passed, approving of Saturday's work, applauding Mr. Bligh as a "gallant hero", and — oh ye Wellingtons, ye Nelsons and Napiers! — deciding that he was entitled to a sword, and that the pleasure of subscribing for it must be limited to 5s per man . . . I still hope "the inhabitants of Maryborough" will repudiate even their own act . . . What honour can there be? — what courage is required? — what noble qualities are displayed in occasionally slaughtering the naked, unarmed, flying savage? . . . 'Twas arrogantly rewarding, for a single act, a personage who had, up to that moment, ostentatiously revelled in idleness, and till then insolently DECLARED his determination to the Maryborough people not to protect them.
>
> I am, &c.,
> "A BELIEVER IN GASSON'S STATEMENT."
> Wide Bay, April 10th, 1861.[66]

Definitely, the Native Mounted Police were everything Jack had claimed — and much more!

Newspaper columns of the day also condemned the Native Mounted Police, their headlines screaming "murderers", "inhuman savages", "kidnappers". The latter disparaging epithet was levelled at the black police because of their lesser known activities of kidnapping black children. The 1902 Report of the Northern Protector of Aborigines states:

> It is known that in the past years a most obnoxious practice grew up of the police supplying their friends etc. with Aboriginal children . . . This "trucking" in children is still going on. "Settlers in outside districts" — I am quoting Protector Galbraith — "who have plenty of myalls about their country are often importuned by town residents and others to bring them in a boy or a girl. In due time the child arrives. How the children are separated from their parents is a subject of conjecture and surmise. Most people will tell you that the child is better off with Europeans: in my opinion the contention is absurd . . . This practice has been going on for years, and, with the exception of one or two cases personally known to me, without good results

> to the children. They change masters and mistresses, prostitution and disease follow . . . and finally become pariahs amongst both whites and blacks.[67]

"Protector" was the title given to a person in whose custody belongings and pay were entrusted — usually the local police officer. The following year, Galbraith stated in his report: "A large number of individuals have an idea that they can trade an Aboriginal as they would a horse or a bullock. Some of these people are church-goers. One lady informed me that an Aboriginal had been left to her by will."[68]

There are many cases documented in which black police supplied young Aboriginal girls to families who then became their "foster parents". In most cases, these young people were kept merely as domestic slaves or made to pander to the male foster parent. Those of whom this "service" was not required nevertheless became the eventual prey of unscrupulous whites. In other cases, older girls were supplied to whites. These youngsters were nothing more than live-in call-girls! The resultant half-caste children were stigmatized by both the black and the white society.

Another method of obtaining women for sexual services was to bribe the elders of a tribe by supplying them with opium. It was not the "good" opium which was supplied but the ashes from the addict's pipe. This was mixed with water and given to the ignorant black to drink. To satisfy his subsequent craving, the elder would supply women — mostly the young girls. These lubras were then exposed to the evils and vices of lowly members of white society. It will be surprising for the reader to learn that some settlers supplied opium to blacks. The Protector in the Northern district states in his report of 1903 that, "It is exceptional to find a station that does not supply it to blacks." In

Queensland, a police officer stated that it was common practice for white employers and employees to round up groups of Aborigines for the sole purpose of despoiling the women. When a raid was carried out on one particular station, each of the unattached men were found to have a young black girl in his bed. The station owner told police that he considered this practice the only means by which he could attract employees. I suppose, in modern day terms, it would be called "fringe benefits"! The practice became so rife that one Aboriginal Protector earnestly suggested that all young girls — black and half-caste — be removed to missions for their own protection because there were many white men waiting either to rape or seduce them. As stated earlier, the further tragedy of these young girls was that the prospective seducer was already infected with venereal disease.

But I diverge. Let's get back to these rotten native troopers. A letter, addressed to the editor of the *Rockhampton Chronicle* by Mr P. Sellheim and published by that newspaper, condoned and defended the actions of the Native Police Force. Sensing a sharp reaction from its readers, the editor added a footnote to Sellheim's letter:

> For the information of our correspondent and to prevent the public from being misled by his statements, we may remark that the letter of which he complains, and most of the correspondence which has appeared on the subject in our columns, emanated from persons engaged in squatting pursuits — some of them in Mr Sellheim's own district — Ed.[69]

The editor of another newspaper, the *Courier*, roundly denounced the actions of the Native Mounted Police:

> But to allow them [blacks] to do mischief on a station, and retire to shelter; then to let slip the black troopers on them, as if the

> latter were bloodhounds, and allow them to pursue the fugitives and murder them in secret places of the scrub, without any distinction of age, or between the innocent and the guilty; we would ask if this is an English, manly, prudent, Christian, enlightened mode of warfare upon naked and neglected heathens? Is it not rather a system of retaliation copied from the customs of all the darkest places of the earth, and those which must abound in deeds of cruelty?

The editor then adds:

> At all events, as a whole, the Native Police Force has proved a failure so far. The experiment of a white police has never been fairly tried, and we have long ago shown that, if a white force could be organized that would prove equally efficient, at anything like the same expense, the advantages accruing to the colony would be ten times as great.[70]

Of course, it depends upon what the editor considered "the advantage to the colony". Did he mean that a white police force would be ten times more efficient? If so, efficient at what? Killing ten times as many blacks? Newspaper editors of the day were very daring and scathing in their editorials — unlike the politically handcuffed editors of today — but, nevertheless, their writings were sometimes most ambiguous. However, it was the editorial in the *Maryborough Chronicle*, dated 4 April 1861, which not only castigated Bligh but also fired the first shots at Lieutenant John Murray of the Native Police Force. As more of the facts emerged, the shots echoed as a cannonade. The first information of the massacre (which took place in Manumbar cattle station, about twenty-two kilometres north-west of Nanango) was reported in the format of an advertisement in the *Moreton Bay Courier* on 16 March 1861. The writer of this advertisement was later to face intensive questioning before the Select Committee enquiring into the Native Police. The advertisement is well worth reproducing.

To the Officer in Command of the Party of of [sic] Native Police, who shot and wounded some blacks on the Station of Manumbar, on Sunday, the 10th instant.

Sir, If in future you should take a fancy to bring your troopers upon the Station of Manumbar on a sporting excursion we shall feel obliged if you would either bag or bury the game which you shoot as it is far from pleasant for us to have the decomposing remains of four or five blackfellows laying unburied within a mile or two of our head station. If you will do neither — please be kind enough to remove the corpses from water-holes near the head station from which we sometimes use water for culinary purposes. As most of the blacks you left dead on our run were feeble old men, some of them apparently not less than eighty years of age, will you please inform us whether these hoary sinners are the party chiefly engaged in spearing bullocks and "cramming monkeys", &c.; or whether you just shoot them because the younger ones are too nimble for you. Besides the four or five you left dead on our run, you have wounded two of our station blacks, who have been in our employment during lambing season, washing, and shearing, and all other busy times for the last eight or nine years, and we have never known either of them to have been charged with a crime of any kind. One of them came to the station with a bullet wound through one of his thighs, another through one of his arms, and another through one of his hands; the other had a bullet wound through one of his arms. These blacks, being in our employment, very naturally look to us for protection from such outrages, and we are of opinion that when you shoot and wound blacks in such an indiscriminate manner, you exceed your commission, and we publish this that those who employ and pay you may have some knowledge of the way in which you perform your services.

We have &c.,
T. & A. Mortimer
Manumbar, Feb. 22, 1860.

An article in the *Maryborough Chronicle*, dated 4 April 1861, exacerbated the affair:

> Whenever an advocate steps forward in favour of the Native Police, it generally happens that something instantly arises to strengthen the universal feeling of condemnation with which that force is regarded . . . The inhabitants of Maryborough — who not long since "delighted to honour" a native police lieutenant to such an extent as to present him with a "handsome cavalry sword" for shooting or capturing a blackfellow or two — are now becoming indignant at the conduct of *another* lieutenant who, together with his troopers, has lately made an onslaught on the aborigines, and is said to have massacred the inmates of a camp indiscriminately. Whatever may be the actual circumstances of the case, we *know* positively that a slaughter has lately taken place in a district contiguous to Wide Bay and if half of the horrors described as attendant upon it have any foundation in fact, civilisation has been again disgraced by a cowardly and cold-blooded deed. It is reported that some thirty or thirty-five blacks — including men, women and children — have been *butchered* — there is no other term for it — by a detachment of native police; and it is further stated that this detachment was under the command of Lieut. Murray . . .[71]

This article alludes to the massacre which took place on Manumbar Station. Actually, Murray was many miles away but this fact, apparently, did not exonerate him from blame because he had detailed his troopers under the command of Sublieutenant Morisset.

Morisset was the young brother of the Commandant of the Native Mounted Police Force whose Headquarters were at Sandgate. Young Morisset had been in the Force for fewer than twelve months and could not, under any circumstances, be regarded as sufficiently qualified to command a detachment of troopers. And so it proved. More than thirty blacks perished needlessly because of Lieutenant Murray's foolish indiscretion. When he was giving evidence at the Select Committee enquiry, the chairman persisted with his questioning of Commandant Morisset on his brother's competence to be in charge of a detachment:

> Q. I again ask — do you think that a young officer should be entrusted with a detachment, and go blazing away into the blacks in that way?[72]

The affray at Manumbar was not the only factor to give the Committee cause to discharge Murray from the Force. Further questions were put to Commandant Morisset by the Chairman:

> Q. Have you seen him [Lieut. Murray] in a state of intoxication?
> A. Yes.
>
> Q. As it is your intention to leave the Force, can you conscientiously recommend that Mr Murray should remain in it, supposing that the present Force is not disbanded?
> A. If he continues in habits of intemperance, he would be unfit to carry out his duties.[73]

When the various actions of the officers of the Force were assessed, Lieutenant Murray received the maximum penalty — dismissal from the Force. The Committee report stated:

> With respect to the affray at Mortimer's, it appears that the detachment of police stationed at Maryborough was most improperly handed over by the Officer in charge, Lieutenant Murray, to Second Lieutenant Morrisset [sic] a young officer newly appointed, unacquainted with his duties, and also with the Troopers placed under his control. It also appears by the evidence that the natives had been committing depredations in the neighbourhood for some time previous, and that the assistance of the police had been demanded. It is likewise shown by Mr Morrisset's [sic] report that they attacked the police in the first instance. After a careful consideration of the evidence in this case, your Committee recommended that Lieutenant Murray should be removed from the Force, both on this account, and general unfitness for his duties.[74]

"They hang a blackfella in Brisbane?"

It was now about three months since I had returned from Urandangie. I was anxious to return to that hot, dusty little place and talk once again with Cyclone Jack. I smiled as I conjured up visions of his gummy smile and his excitement as I related the information about the Native Mounted Police Force. I imagined how he would swell with pride as I told him about police officers such as Bligh, Wheeler and Murray. I could hear him saying, "See, I told you so, eh?"

There was really no need for me to stay in Brisbane any longer. I was tired of watching the boring old shows on television; there always seemed to be someone getting shot, knifed, smashed up in a car or being blown sky-high! I could not escape it. The volume of the neighbour's radio seemed to mysteriously increase when some unpleasant news item was being broadcast. The newspapers screamed in heavily-inked headlines, inexorably dragging one's eyes to some ghastly event. The football season was over. Why not head for the mulga once more?

My small caravan, which I had left in the back yard of a friend here in Brisbane, was overgrown with weeds and grass so I decided to extricate it and drag it back to Urandangie with me. It would be quite a haul for my Datsun 1600 but it would afford some degree of comfort in the bush. I had a small generator which, I hoped, would supply me with occasional refrigeration and light. My mind now made up, it took me no time to chuck a few things into the van and, after waving furiously to a few friends, I very cautiously rolled onto the Pacific Highway. The trip was uneventful except for the usual flat tyre, boiling radiator and broken (not completely) windscreen.

As I approached Jack's hut I could see his scraggy beard lifted in curiosity in my direction. He was still clad in the ragged old dustcoat and oversized trousers. As he recognised me, he almost flung himself off his feet as he waved to me.

"Hey," he yelled. "You here? You back again. You bloody mad, you bastard!" He bared his blackened gums in a smile.

"G'day, Jack," I smiled back. "Hasn't that bottle-brush brew killed you yet? You must have cast-iron guts!" I hopped out and we held each other warmly. I could have counted every rib in his body.

"By gees," he waved towards the caravan. "What you got there? Little 'ouse, eh?" He ran his hand down the wall of the van, tapping it.

"That's my old van," I replied. "I've had it for years. It's a wonder it didn't rattle to bits on the way up here."

A crowd of about twelve Aborigines had gathered around the van and proceeded to rub the dust off the stick-on Aboriginal flag on each side of the Datsun. Cyclone Jack smiled broadly as he touched me on the arm.

"This is my mate," he told the crowd. "Him bin down dere to the town." It amused me that, when Jack got excited, he spoke with a heavy trace of "lingo".

The young man to whom I had given the tin-opener walked up to me.

"Ah, we know dat," he said, scornfully looking at Jack. "You not da only one."

"He bin down and look for some books for me," Jack fired back at the lad. "You don't know. You dumb bastard."

"Hey, Jack," I said to him. "What's this 'bin' business? You learning blackfella talk or something?"

He smiled at me as he scratched his beard. "Ah," he nodded towards the group. "Talking to this mob here. They talk stupid." He turned to his friends and playfully poked out his tongue at them. The mob almost doubled up with laughter at Jack's words and actions.

I looked around for a suitable spot to park the caravan. About a hundred metres from Jack's hut was an old gnarled wild apple tree, its lower limbs about three metres from the ground. I warned the mob to stand well clear as I was not too clever in backing a caravan. They almost knocked each other over in their desire to comply with my warning, eyes bulging and arms flailing in their haste to clear the truck. They were a humorous lot of buggers and I could not help laughing. I considered myself very fortunate to have such good friends way up here in this God-forsaken place. It took only a short time to park the van in a suitable position. After all, I had about fifteen advisers who were shouting instructions — most of them useless and sometimes dangerous — and pointing in different directions.

"How's that fire of yours going, Jack?" I enquired. I began walking towards his hut. As I did so, the mob began to disperse, still debating whether or not the van was parked in the most suitable position.

"Fire no good," Jack admitted. "I got no wood in. I'll get some from that old tree there." He pointed across the paddock.

"She's right, Jack," I called to him as I returned to the van. He turned and followed me over.

"What would you like, Jack, tea or coffee?"

"Aw, I'll have tea, Bill," he replied, following me into the van. He wriggled himself in behind the small folding table and settled himself.

"You sure you wouldn't like some of that bottle-brush piss you drink?" I jibed him.

Jack doubled himself up with laughter. It was really good to hear his wheezy laugh once again. "I got none left," he answered. "But now that you're back, I'll get some more."

The perfect squelch! I gave him the fingers and he almost choked with laughter. The water boiled quickly and I made the tea. As he sipped his tea, he looked around the van.

"Like a little 'ouse," he observed. "You've got bed, stove, everything."

Before I sat down I opened a cupboard and removed a manila file and placed it on the table between us. Jack's eyes alternated from the file to me.

"You were right, you old bugger," I said, as I took out a sheaf of photostat pages and placed them on the table.

His eyes squinted as he gazed at them, then he held a page close to his eyes. I remained silent and still, quietly enjoying my tea. As I watched him, his face took on many shapes. His lips were drawn deeply into his mouth. Suddenly, he exploded!

"Dere! Look dere. Wheeler. Where you bin get this . . ." He looked across at me, realising he was getting carried away and that his pronunciation was faulty.

"Where did you find this?" he corrected himself, still trying hard to control his excitement.

"I don't know where I found that particular page," I replied. "I've been to many places since I last saw you."

"Where you been?" A puzzled look crossed his face.

"Aw, struth!" I exclaimed. "All over the place; the Mitchell Library in Sydney; the Institute Library in Canberra; State Archives; Oxley Library; the Historical Socie . . ."

"Look out," Jack interrupted. "I don't know them places. I'm sorry I asked." He turned the page around to me and placed a long, grimy fingernail onto it.

"See," he said, jubilantly. "What did I tell you?" The particular printed matter on the page which had caused him such excitement referred to an Appendix to Dr Henry Challinor's evidence which he had given to the Select Committee enquiry. (Challinor was the Magistrate for the Ipswich district.) It read, in part:

> I shall be able to produce additional evidence, if required; but as the shooting of the said blacks is now distinctly and unequivocally traced to Lieutenant Wheeler and the detachment of Native Police under his command, on the 24th day of December last, it appeared to me that I might close the present enquiry.[75]

Jack read it and re-read it out loud, sometimes stumbling over the words but he was quite aware of what they meant. He placed the papers back onto the table.

"Bastard!" he said, in a quiet, controlled voice. His flash of anger quickly passed. He seemed pleased that, at last, the word was out. He would no longer have to tell his story to listeners whose tongues clicked meaninglessly. Here it was — in black and white. He cast his eyes down to the pages once more, a blank, neutral expression covering his face. What was he thinking? Was he thinking about the massacre of his grandfather's camp? . . . the water turning red as his granduncle lay on the coarse sand of Christmas Creek, his life's blood draining away? . . . perhaps it was the shot which brutally crippled his father and his grandfather and the mad, desperate rush to climb up and out of danger. There could be no doubt, however, that the name "Wheeler", the name which had been burned into his consciousness since he was old enough to remember, figured prominently in his thoughts.

When his conscious mind returned to the present, he drank the remainder of his tea which was now quite cold. I offered to heat it up for him but he declined.

"I like it cold," he told me. "It's easier on my throat. What else did you find out, Bill?"

"Oh, a whole lot of stuff," I answered. "I'm sick of looking at it all. Some of it is pretty gruesome stuff."

I removed the rest of the files from the cupboard and placed them onto the table in front of Jack.

"Here," I invited. "Go for your life."

He stacked the files tidily on one end of the table and drew out a page. At about 6.00 p.m., I started up the generator and Cyclone Jack's eyes opened wide in amazement as the inside of the van became flooded in brilliant light. I sat with Jack for several hours, alternately reading and watching the changing expressions on Jack's face. I made a mug of coffee for us both at 9.00 p.m. and, as Jack made no signs of moving an hour later, I rolled into bed and left him to his own devices.

At six o'clock the following morning, Jack thumped on my door.

"Don't you ever sleep?" I called out, good-humouredly. I rose and, by way of an unbreakable habit, the first thing I did was to put on the water for a cup of tea. Jack came inside and sat where he had sat the previous night. His hair and beard were a mess!

"That seat must be still warm," I teased.

He did not reply; instead, he reached for the bundle of files and untied the string.

"There's a few things here I don't understand," he frowned. "You'll have to explain them to me."

I poured out the tea and pushed a mug over to him. "No problem," I assured him. "What's worrying you?"

"Well, there's this blackfella called Gullee . . . Gull . . . How you say that name?"

I took the page from him and glanced at what he was reading. He looked at me expectantly.

"Ah, yes," I began to explain. "That's Gull . . . liv-va." I said the word phonetically for him.

"Well, this Gull . . . ivva . . . I can't make out what happened to him. You know?"

"Yes," I answered. "I think so. Well, this Gulliver was a bit of a bad bugger, I think. For a start, he was once a trooper in your infamous Native Police. He was suspected of being involved in the murder of a white woman called Fanny Briggs. It is generally believed that it was the Native Police troopers who murdered her. Understand?"

"Mmmm," Jack answered, unconvincingly, "I'll catch on."

"OK, Gulliver was taken to Rockhampton but he later got away. The story goes that he headed back to his own country . . . around the Dawson River area. One day he saw one of his old mates from his trooper days called Kennis. Well, Jack, old Gulliver made a bad blue there. See, there were a couple of draymen there, too — a drayman was a man who earned his living by carting things from one place to another," I explained to him. "With me so far?"

"Yair, yair. Go on," his eyes were riveted on my lips, hardly daring to breathe.

"Now, these two draymen got poor old Gulliver drunk and they tied him up to one of the drays. It wasn't long before the troopers rode up. Their Commanding Officer was with them. He was Lieutenant Powell. The police took Gulliver away. A witness at the Select Committee, a bloke called Babbit, said that the troopers took Gulliver into the bush and when he asked what had become of him, he was told that it was 'one of those things which ought not to be talked about'.[76] Henry Babbit was a map salesman who travelled extensively throughout the district."

Cyclone Jack sat bolt upright, his mouth gaping. "You mean, they shot him?"

"That's the general belief," I told him. "Although there were a lot of people who reckoned he escaped — that he was allowed to escape. No one can really say for sure. It's just another of those little mysteries."[77]

Jack sat quietly, his beard clutched firmly in his hand. He shook his head but said nothing. Although I had plenty of information with me, I was unaware of how he would understand the significance of it. He turned his attention once more to the pile of paper upon the table and began to read. He flipped the pages over slowly as he read each one, and his floppy lips never stopped moving. I sat watching his reactions, supplying him with lighted cigarettes as he chain-smoked.

A sudden frown creased his forehead as he pointed to a page he was reading.

"This here, Bill," he enquired. "What's this? They hang a blackfella in Brisbane?"

"They hanged a few blacks in Brisbane. Which one are talking about?" I took the page from him and studied it. "Yes," I informed him, as I recognised the photostat. "That's a blackfellow called Dundalli. He was hanged alright. He was hanged right at the spot where the Brisbane General Post Office now stands."

"What for?"

"Murder," I replied. "He and another blackfellow called Jemmy — Millbong Jemmy — killed some people down near the Pine River, near Brisbane.[78] Dundalli was caught at a place which is now the corner of Wickham and Brunswick Streets. By the way," I broke my narrative, "the name 'Dundalli' means Wonga pigeon." Jack was unimpressed with my knowledge of Aboriginal names. I think I gave him a dirty look before continuing. "When Dundalli was hanged, they made the rope too long and he smashed into the ground. The fall didn't kill him so the hangman had to swing on his legs until he choked to death."

Jack swallowed hard. "Hmmm," he said, at last. "That other fella, Millbong? That's a funny name, eh?"

"Yes," I agreed. "But he wasn't a very funny bloke."

Jack's eyes were transfixed upon me. I knew that look by now. Whenever I made an off-beat statement like that he fully expected me to elaborate.

"No," I began. "He was a bit of a menace. His real name was Yilbong. The word 'Yilbong' means 'one-eyed' and he was called that for a reason. He . . ."

"He only had one eye," Jack interrupted, smirking at his powers of deduction.

"Picked it in one," I commended him. "You'd put Sherlock Holmes out of a job."

"Who's that?"

"Forget it!" I waved his question aside. "Millbong's other eye was burnt out when he was a kid," I continued. "It was probably some form of punishment for some breach of custom. He might have looked up a girl's dress, or something." I immediately felt stupid at my hasty surmise because they didn't *have* dresses in those days. I was thankful Jack didn't pick me up on that.

"Anyway, Millbong — or Yilbong, if you like — was a pretty smart cookie. He could recite the Lord's prayer, no problem. One day he was caught pinching corn meal and he was sentenced to twenty-five lashes and twenty-four hours in jail. As soon as he was let out of jail he started stealing again. He nicked some tobacco and swapped it for a bag of sweet potatoes. He told Tom Petrie — you don't know him, either! — that he saw no harm in stealing because the white man had 'taken his country' and they 'should give something for it'."

"Fair enough." Jack said precisely what I expected him to say. He looked at me with a mischievous grin.

"Sounds like he might have been the first black demonstrator." He sniggered a little then pushed my arm. "Well, go on," he urged. "What happened to him?"

"Do you really want to know?" I asked him. "It's pretty bloody horrible."

He did not answer for a few moments. "Aw, yair," he said. "You better tell me or I'll lie awake all bloody night thinkin' about what might have happened."

"Ah, well," I began. "One day a couple of timber-cutters tricked Millbong into having some tea with them. They were after the reward money for him so, when Millbong's attention was diverted, one of the men shot him in the head. Tom Petrie avers that his head was cut off and 'boiled free of flesh' so a cast could be made of it. Gruesome?"[79]

"Aw, shit." Jack expressed his favourite vulgarism, with feeling.

For a while, I thought he was going to vomit. His Adam's apple slid up and down at a fast rate and he compressed his lips. I got up off my seat in readiness to propel him out the door with some dispatch but he held up a reassuring finger. He licked his chops several times and went back to his reading. Each time he recognised some happening or name which, perhaps, his father had told him about, he would bend closer to the pages, an occasional "Ssss" or "Hmmm" escaping his lips. He reached out and touched me lightly on the arm.

"Bill," he said, a deep frown crossing his face. "I remember a name Walker. Walker. Walker. My father say. I think of this f'la after you go. You heard of him?"

"Yes," I replied, "as a matter of fact, I have. He was in the Native Police Force. Actually he was the Commandant." I waited for Jack's next move. I knew he would not be able to contain himself for long. He did not disappoint me.

"Well," he said, impatiently. "Go on! Bloody well tell me about him."

I laughed out loudly at his boyish anxiety. "Walker had the same name as your old mate, Wheeler," I told him. "His name was Frederick, too. He was a real pisspot. There were times he was so drunk, he couldn't sit on his horse. He went arse-over-head off a few times. Well, the government got wind of his drinking habits and called an enquiry. They ordered Walker to attend. He attended alright; so drunk that he didn't even know who was in the courtroom.[80] Even his troopers were so ashamed of him that they left him. Anyway, they had to adjourn the enquiry. It was found that he was fiddling government money, too. He would draw funds to buy tucker for the troopers but he never used to."

"What did he do with it, then?"

"Got drunk, I suppose," I replied. "When you think about it, he would be about as good as a sore arse to a jockey."

"Eh?"

"Forget it, Jack," I said, quickly. "It ended up with the officers having to buy tucker for the troopers out of their own pockets. The government stopped giving him money in the end. A Board of Enquiry considered that he was 'in constant habit of intoxication that rendered him totally unfit for any responsible post under Government, and particularly for that of commanding the Native Police'.[81] They sacked him in the end."[82]

"Served the bastard right," commented Jack.

"Being sacked didn't stop him," I explained. "Walker organised his own band of private troopers. But after a while, the government made him disband it because they considered it to be an illegal force."

"What did they do?"

"Got rid of it. Sacked the lot."

"That stopped him eh?"

"Not quite," I replied. "Years later, in 1861, he led an expedition from Rockhampton in search of the missing Burke and Wills. He died at a place called Floraville — in the Gulf country — on 19 November 1866."[83]

Even though Lieutenant Frederick Walker had been

a member of the Native Police, the establishment for which Jack held so much hatred, talk of his death affected Jack. Even though he would be unable to express his feelings, Jack recognised death as the great leveller.

Jack went back to his reading, and was so engrossed that he did not notice me leave the van. I left him sitting there, a half-packet of cigarettes on the table, and wandered across to a couple of Aborigines as they waved to me from their camp near the windmill. I spent a few minutes talking to them and then continued on my way down to the river and sat under some huge she-oaks. To sit alone in the bush has a most pacifying effect. All is quiet and still — except for the occasional rustle of the trees as a wandering breeze momentarily fraternises with them, or the anxious "twit" of a bird as it cocks its head, wondering if this interloper is some strange predator. I must have dozed off in the warm sun. When I awoke, the sun was hidden behind a bank of ominous black cloud. The breeze had turned quite chilly. When I returned to the van, Jack was no longer there but the files were stacked neatly against the wall and beside them was an empty cigarette packet. The sky was now heavily overcast and it was quite dark. I replenished the generator with fuel and set it going. On hearing the engine, Jack came to the door. I invited him in and waved him to his seat.

"Well, Jack," I asked, "did you have a good read?"

"Too right, Bill," Jack grinned. As he looked at me his grin changed to a frown. "I don't understand that part about that naked woman," he confessed. "Can't get the gist of that at all."

"Naked woman!" I replied, matching his frown. "What naked woman? What are you talking about?

You living in hopes, or something?" He smiled coyly at my remark.

"No, Bill," he laughed. "Not me." He darted his hand into the heap of files and withdrew one of them.

"Here." He handed me the manila cover. I recognised his misunderstanding.

"Ah, Jack," I teased him. "You had me all excited there for a while."

"Hey!" Jack scolded playfully. "You thinking dirty."

I laughed dutifully at his remark. He was happy. The subject matter to which he was referring was a most interesting tale told by Michael Terry in his book, *War of the Warramullas*.[84]

"I can't understand it," Jack complained. "I don't know how to put the words."

"It's really a beautiful story of a man's love for a woman."

He looked at me with a vacant expression.

"Would you like me to read it to you?" I offered.

"Aw, Bill, that would be real good." He put his hands together in a silent clap, much like a little boy might at his mother's promise to tell him a fairy story. I sat down opposite and began to read:

> . . . After we had eaten, O'Neill took us to a place in the desert scrub where two Aborigines were sitting. One was a fine young man — he would have been a warrior had he been with his tribe — wearing only a sort of sporran of pearl shell. Beside him sat a young girl, aged about twelve. She was his child wife and her name was Kuluin [meaning black swan]. Her nakedness, from shoulder to half-way down her thighs, was covered only by a singlet. Between these two was a love that women the world over might envy. At a word from O'Neill, Kuluin's husband, Jimmy, lifted his wife's singlet and showed us her back. As a youngster in the First World War and even during my desert wanderings, I had become used to wounds and the agony that

can come to flesh. But now I was shocked and touched almost to tears. Almost all of the girl's back and the backs of her arms were terribly burnt. The flesh was scarred and wrinkled and distorted and still blistering from burning. The flesh of the left elbow was burnt nearly to the bone. I think a white child of Kuluin's age would have died under the torture and injury she must have undergone. But Kuluin sat in the red sand, mute and appealing, yet full of courage. Jimmy let the singlet fall into place and we turned away, feeling quite sick. I knew the girl was scarred for life and I thought she might not use her left elbow again. This was Jimmy's story. He and Kuluin were camped somewhere in the Schist Hills, not far from the Granites. At nightfall, while they were burning spinifex to keep warm, Kuluin's clothing caught fire, and she was terribly burnt before Jimmy could tear the garments from her. He opened an artery in his arm and allowed the blood to pour over the burned flesh, believing it would ease her pain. The he made mud and smeared it over her back as a salve, in the Aboriginal manner. Jimmy must have lost much blood from the opened artery, for he told us that his strength had ebbed. Kuluin could not possibly walk. Shock and pain had left her semi-conscious. Unless she could be got to white man's help she would surely die. Yet the nearest white men known to Jimmy were O'Neill and his mates, sixty miles away. So he took his girl-wife in his arms and began to walk, and without food and water he carried her for three days and three nights. One blazing sunset he arrived at O'Neill's camp. Kuluin herself was by then delirious from thirst as well as from her wounds. O'Neill gave them both water in carefully measured doses. Then, leaving Jimmy in his own camp, he took the girl to the police camp at Tanami where Hood treated her. Fortunately he had a good supply of boracic powder. After that, with care and feeling, Kuluin began to recover. The only part of Jimmy's story which is probably not true is how Kuluin received her terrible burns. They did not look like the widespread but fairly superficial burns that would have been caused by a shirt or singlet catching fire. We white men believed at the time, and I still believe, that the girl had offended against some tribal law, and had been deliberately held over a fire by tribal elders. If this is the truth, Jimmy's devotion to his little Kuluin was even greater. For, in taking her away from the tribe after she had undergone torture, and risking his own life by carrying her

> across sixty miles of desert, he laid himself open to punishment by tribal magic. There was a happy ending to this remarkable love story of the desert. I returned to Tanami two years later and Kuluin and Jimmy were still there. The girl had recovered as only the Aboriginal can. True, her back was still scarred. But her face, which had been beautiful in the muteness of her pain, was beautiful in a new way — she had a baby of her own.

Jack's face seemed to melt. He remained silent and motionless for some time before he rose from his seat.

"By gees, that's nice, that," he remarked, as he carefully lowered himself out of the van.

"That girl," he frowned deeply. "I wonder what she done." He took a few paces towards his hut and stopped, his fingers twisting the ends of his beard.

"Must have been bad thing," he mused. "Very bad thing."

He reappeared in a little while, still adjusting his fly. I began re-reading the story I had just narrated to Jack when there was a knock on the door.

"Hey, you there, Bill?" It was Ruby and her mob of friends. They came into the van and sat on the floor.

"Well, what have you jokers been up to today?" I asked. "I haven't seen you for hours."

"Aw, we bin chasin' them cattle," replied a young member of the group. His eyes were bright and conveyed the fun — or mischief! — they had been up to. "We have good fun," he continued. "Some ob us run 'em dere an' den dem udder f'la chase 'em back."

"You let that bloody grazier — the joker that owns them — catch you, he'll hack your knackers out!" I warned him. "You're running all the condition off them."

He gave an "I don't care" look. We all yarned on for several hours, talking about the condition of the land, the amount of "blackfella" tucker — or lack of it —

available around the bush. I put forward my view that there was stacks of tucker around.

"Aw, no," they assured me. "Not much dere. Nuttin'."

"Balls!" I responded. "That's got to be a load of bullshit. When I looked over to the other side of the river yesterday morning, all I could see were kangaroos. There were hundreds of them."

"Got no rifle," came the lame excuse.

"Well, do what your fathers did, spear them."

They looked at each other and grinned. After further discussion it occurred to me that they did not know how to *make* a spear. Indeed, Aboriginal know-how was fast becoming a nonentity. They could explain the theory to me — just as their fathers did to them — but there was no way in the world they could make a spear. Whatever would this young generation do if given land rights, the concept with which I agree and wholeheartedly support. But it came to my mind that this current generation would need an ample supply of tinned camp pie and an adequate supply of opening devices.

"But we bin catch gwanna," one of them defended.

"Sure," I argued. "But you can't live on bloody goannas all your life."

As I finished speaking, a groan came from Ruby. She began rubbing her knee and grimacing with pain.

"This knee is killing me," she moaned. I looked at it and saw that it was badly swollen.

"We'll go back home tomorrow," I told her. "You will have to have that knee treated or you won't be able to chase any more kangaroos. Your dog will starve."

I tried to make light of Ruby's situation but, clearly, she was in pain. She smiled at my attempt. Cyclone Jack would be all right now. I would leave the photostat copies of the archival papers with him. He would be happy.

"We'll leave tomorrow, about eleven o'clock. How's that?"

She gave a sigh of relief. I could not leave earlier as I had the Datsun jacked up and was in the process of replacing the universal joint. It would not take me too long to slap the bits together providing they all fitted. I have always been hexed by the fact that, when I fix a car (or a tape recorder), I always seem to have pieces left over.

"Well," Ruby said, "I'm off to bed."

The entire group rose from their various positions on the floor with such haste that they almost tumbled poor old Jack out of the door. The old man had gone into a doze and was startled at all the sudden movement.

"Oooo, shit. What's wrong?" he yelped.

We all laughed loudly at the poor old bugger's confused state. Within seconds, they had all gone out into the night.

The following morning I spoke to Jack and reminded him that I would be leaving soon. He was disappointed that we could not spend many more hours together, just yarning away. He was a wonderful old bloke, in spite of his ragged and unkempt appearance. I toyed with the idea of taking him back with me and, perhaps, looking after him in some sort of way. But I knew that would be unwise because I would be spending a lot of my time either travelling or working away from home. Relucantly, I dismissed the idea.

"Ah, I'm a bit tired," he stifled a yawn.

"Don't you sleep at night?" I joked.

"Not much," was his brief reply. He seemed haggard and clumsy as he went over to his favourite sleeping spot under the clump of stunted trees. He lowered himself down gently and made himself comfortable.

"I'll see you before I go," I said to him as I walked towards the jacked-up Datsun. He waved a bent arm to me. I crawled under the ute and replaced the worn part and, amazingly, all the bits fitted where the book said they would. I was further surprised to find that there were no bolts left over.

After I had cleaned up I yarned on with the "mill mob", as I now called to them, then Ruby and I jumped into the ute and went over to Jack's hut to say goodbye to him.

To my consternation, I noticed he was still lying in the same position as when I last saw him.

"Hey, Jack," I yelled to him. "I'm just about ready to leave. I'll see you when I get back."

He did not move. I went closer to him and a sudden fear overtook me. I bent down and shook him gently but he did not respond.

Old Cyclone Jack was dead!

The light breeze played with his wispy, snow-white hair. The dust had somehow fallen from his beard leaving it slate grey yet heavily flecked with snow. As he lay there, his lifeless skin exposed the mould of his bones and his lips were drawn back in a toothless snarl.

My mind went back to the hours Jack and I had spent, just yarning away the hours and drinking tea or coffee — whichever had the most colour in it. I recalled his agitation whenever I was loath to believe him; and his yellowed eyes as they opened wide to emphasise a particular point in his narrative; his lips, when they would suddenly disappear into his toothless mouth as he narrated the stories which created humour, horror and a deep sense of injustice in my mind. But his frail old heart was stilled now. He would never again concern himself with the "Wheelers", the "Blighs" or any other facet of the Native Mounted Police Force, the spectre of which had been so indelibly etched into his brain.

I peered inside the hut and looked at his frugal belongings — the old broken mattress, the two fragile pine boxes upon which we had sat until a few short hours ago, the battered old billy. But what distressed me most of all were the cold, smoke-blackened stones of the fire. How wretched and forlorn it all was.

I went back outside and my eyes stung as I looked down at his form. I drew the old threadbare blanket over his vacant stare. Was I looking at the last vestige of the beleaguered Telemon tribe?

I turned and, as I walked towards the Datsun, I recalled once more the corroboree song he had sung for me when we first met. That ridiculous voice he had teased me into thinking was the real thing. The old bugger! That wonderful, harmless, lovable old bugger.

This is the story of that old bugger.

Appendix

Extracts from Queensland Legislative Assembly Minutes of Evidence taken before The Select Committee on The Native Police Force and the Conditions of the Aborigines in General (Chairman: The Honorable R.R. Mackenzie)

WEDNESDAY 8 MAY 1861

Dr Henry Challinor, MP

1. By the Chairman: You are the Coroner of the Police District of Ipswich? I am.

2. I find that on the third and fourth of January last you instituted a Magisterial Enquiry at Fassifern respecting the death of some blacks, — did you hold a Magisterial, and NOT a Coroner's Inquest then, or did you on any subsequent occasion? I held a Magisterial Enquiry on the third of January — an enquiry commencing on the third, and adjourned to the fourth, and subsequently to other dates, which I can't remember just now, but the date was put to each of the depositions.

3. There was an adjourned enquiry from time to time? Yes.

4. But did you, at the time you held the first enquiry at Fassifern, see the bodies — will you explain why you did not hold an inquest in the regular way, instead of making a Magisterial Enquiry? In the first place I knew it was illegal to hold an inquest on bodies lightly putrified. I had received information as early as the Monday preceding Christmas Day — the day before Christmas day — that some blacks had been shot in the paddock of Mr. Hardie, of Fassifern.

13. Now, with regard to what occurred at Fassifern — you received certain information, and proceeded to act upon it? I did.
14. Will you state what you saw — what came under your own observation? I observed three dead blackfellows, — one of the bodies was considerably burned; two of them I recognised as being old men, because they were grey-headed, — one in particular had a grey beard.
15. Did you know them at all — had you ever seen them? I did not know them.
16. There were three, I think you stated? There were three; and the bodies were so highly decomposed, that when we came to examine them and to turn them over, they fell to pieces; they were lying on their backs, and when we came to move the bodies for the purpose of examining the under surface, the parts would not hold together.
17. Did you notice any particular wounds in the bodies of these blacks? The skulls of two of them had been fractured, and there were what appeared to be bullet wounds on the body.
18. Do you consider that the evidence brought before you was sufficiently conclusive to warrant you in assuming that Lieutenant Wheeler was the cause of death in the case of these blacks? I do.
19. What was your reason for coming also to the assumption that some of the witnesses as to the death of these blacks did not give their evidence correctly on oath? I may be allowed to state that the question enters into my conduct as Coroner, and I dispute the right of the Committee to enquire into my conduct as Coroner. I am quite prepared to defend it before a Committee empowered to do so; but I don't think it falls within the power of this Committee to make these enquiries; I therefore decline to answer the question.
20. You have stated in your letter to the Attorney-General that "the shooting of the said blacks is now distinctly and unequivocally traced to Lieutenant Wheeler, and the detachment of the Native Police under his command, on the 24th day of December last" — *(vide* Appendix. Letter of Dr. Challinor to the Honorable the Attorney-General, January 29th, 1861) — **I now ask you, how have you come to that conclusion?** From the depositions — the sworn depositions.

22. I want to know how you came to the assumption that the whites on that occasion gave false testimony — you speak (*vide* Appendix) **of your "information being derived from two perfectly independent sources," but**

that has nothing to do with the sworn evidence? I think I have stated that I came to the conclusion from the sworn depositions which I forwarded to the Attorney-General; but, beyond that, I don't think that this Committee has any power to ask me any questions on this subject.

37. [By Mr. Watts] Did you see the whole of the three blacks lying dead at Fassifern yourself? I saw the three blacks; they were all highly decomposed, but one was considerably charred, and consumed (by fire).
38. From the appearance of the bodies were you led to believe that they were shot, or do you think, from the wounds in the heads, or whatever appeared on the bodies, that they could have died from other causes? I believe that they could not have died from any other cause than from injuries inflicted by bullets.
39. From gun-shot wounds? From gun-shot wounds.
40. Was any one present with you at the time you viewed the bodies? Mr. Balbi was with me. I received information that his black knew where the bodies were, and I called at Mr. Balbi's for the black to act as a guide, and to request that Mr. Balbi would come with me as interpreter between us, and that he might direct me to the spot.
41. Can you give any information to the Committee as to what brought the Native Police that came on to the station at Fassifern? Mr. Hardie stated in evidence that he had been speaking to his neighbours — among others I am not certain whether he referred to Mr. Lester, but to some of his neighbours, and that they recommended him to send for the Native Police; and I think it appears in Mr. Hardie's evidence that Mr. Wheeler had been informed at Coochin that Mr. Hardie wanted to see him to disperse the blacks; I think you will find it in Mr. Hardie's evidence.

44. I want to know whether you have any knowledge of their habits and pursuits — of course I want to know your general opinion of the blacks, and what can be done to ameliorate their present position? I think that they ought to be entitled to hunt game on the runs on which they have always done so. I think they should be allowed to procure food on the grounds on which they have been accustomed to procure it; to hunt and fish, unless the Government, in lieu of that, gave them some compensation in the way of food. I say this, because I could produce evidence of cases in which I know that quiet blacks have been molested when fishing, and also when they have been camped on alienated land. In the latter instance their dogs were shot, and blankets and opossum rugs collected and burnt; in the former, they were fishing in the Bundamba Lagoon, and were chased away by dogs and by a man or men on horseback, with stock-whips. I do not state this on my personal knowledge, but I have it from persons who observed the circumstance; I rode fifteen miles to ascertain the correctness of the account in relation to the fishing from a person who saw the occurrence, and forwarded that information to the Sydney Government.

56. [By the Chairman] Do you consider yourself competent to make any suggestions, from your knowledge of the habits of the blacks? Only that they should be allowed to procure food in the way they have been accustomed to do, or that the Government should find them some compensation.

57. Has it come to your knowledge that the blacks are prevented from hunting where they are accustomed? I have heard it.

58. You don't know it from your own knowledge? I know they have been hunted off one station.

APPENDIX TO DR. CHALLINOR'S EVIDENCE

January 29th, 1861.

SIR,

In transmitting you the proceedings of the Magisterial Enquiry respecting the death of the three aboriginals, who were lying dead in the scrub, adjoining the head station, Fassifern, on the 3rd and 4th days of January instant, it is my duty to state that the evidence of Mrs. Hardie did not correspond with the information I received respecting the extent of her knowledge in reference to the death of the said aboriginals. My information was derived from two perfectly independent sources, and the information from these distinct sources was substantially the same. Mr. Hardie's statement about the blackfellow he saw dead, looking as if he had been killed "by a heavy-metalled waddy," the fighting of blackfellows with each other, and the blacks' dogs chasing the horses in the paddocks, are of a piece with the denial of any blacks having been shot on Fassifern station. The story about the rape committed on the daughter of one of the shepherds by two blackfellows eighteen months ago, may or may not be true; but after the false statement he made respecting the shooting of the aboriginals on the 24th of December last, I should hesitate to believe it on his testimony alone. Moreover, when I questioned him on the 12th instant about the service of the first summons I sent to James Bennett, he distinctly told me, as he had told Constable Carson on the 10th instant, that he was not then in his employment, for he had discharged him. Yet, from Bennett's own statement, he had been unremittingly attending a flock of sheep, which Mr. Hardie put under his care on the 26th or 27th of December last, till he was relieved on the 25th instant, that he might appear before me on the following day. I shall be able to produce additional evidence, if required; but as the shooting of the said blacks is now distinctly and unequivocally traced to Lieutenant Wheeler and the detachment of the Native Police under his command, on the 24th day of December last, it appeared to me that I might close the present enquiry. As no committal can take place under this enquiry, but the evidence will have to be re-taken before the persons implicated, I venture respectfully to request that this important case may not be left to be conducted by non-professional men. The Nelson referred to in Farrington's evidence is not the Nelson against whom there is a warrant out for murdering the German woman on her road to Brisbane from the Logan.

I have the honor to be, Sir,
Your obedient Servant.
HENRY CHALLINOR, J.P.

To, the Honourable the Attorney-General,
Brisbane.

THURSDAY 9 MAY 1861

Dr Henry Challinor, MP

3. [By Mr. Ferrett] In speaking of the dead blacks at Fassifern, did I understand you to say that the skulls of two of them were fractured? Yes; two of them had their skulls fractured, and one had not.
4. Did it appear to you that the skulls had been fractured by gun-shot wounds? One of them was considerably destroyed by the fire.
5. And what appearance did the other present? The same appearance as the one at the Dugandan Scrub, the front part of which was all fractured and the bones displaced, and the exit wound could clearly be traced on the other side; I have no doubt the same cause produced the wounds in each case.
6. Now you have mentioned the Dugandan Scrub, were not these blacks all at the Dugandan Scrub? No; there were blacks killed on two different days. On the Friday the blacks were shot at the Dugandan Scrub, near where the road passes from the Peak Mountain Station; that was on the Friday before Christmas Day; the other blacks were shot on the Monday before Christmas Day. The camp at Fassifern was within sight of

the head station, and the bodies were only a few paces, one of them about 15 or 20 paces, from the edge of the scrub.

10. . . . Did I understand you to say that three blacks were shot in the scrub near Fassifern? Yes.
11. I believe I also understood you to say that, as far as you could learn, no provocation had been given by the blacks in that locality? Yes, at the time they were shot. There was nothing in the evidence given before me which led me to believe that any provocation had been given.
12. Did you not say something about huts having been pulled down and robbed, and blankets taken away, and also that Mr. Hardie said his bullocks had been speared and hunted by the blacks? Yes; but not on that day.

30. [By Mr. Moffatt] Was any allusion made yesterday to the affray at Dugandan? I was asked some questions about it, but I do not recollect what they were.
31. Do you recollect how many bodies were found there upon that occasion? It was said there were two, but I only found one.
32. What was the appearance presented by that body? It was injured, evidently by gun-shot wounds. I may say that besides those killed there were other blacks wounded.
33. Did you see them? Yes; I attended one of them who had received a gun-shot wound. In one case, the bullet appeared to have glanced round the rib, and come out at the shoulder blade, or else penetrated the chest. Another shot had fractured his finger. He had his child in his arms when he received the wound in his chest, and the ball grazed the child's shoulder. That man recovered. Another elderly man, I think must have received two balls — one of the wounds at the back of the arm, above the elbow, appeared like an exit wound; the other was in front, and appeared to be an entrance wound; the elbow-joint was fractured, and the ball had traversed down the fore arm, and lodged in the palm of the hand; the head had come away, and the arm below the fractured part was completely dead, and would come away also, if he lived long enough. His thighs were not thicker than my arm. He had scarcely any strength, and but for the sustentation afforded him by the Hospital Committee he could never have lived so long. The last I heard of him, he was recovering, but he was a most pitiable object.
34. Did you hear of any provocation given by those blacks? No.

47. Are you of opinion that they ought to be considered credible witnesses? I must say, the statements made by the blacks before me, in reference to the affair at the scrub leading to Dugandan, were of such a nature that I could not entertain a doubt of them. I never heard evidence given with more care, or with less exaggeration.

48. What test had you of the accuracy of that evidence? Several of the statements were corroborated by the evidence of other witnesses. Some of the blacks who were shot at and wounded in the scrub were asked whether Mr. Wheeler was with his troop at the time, and they said they had not seen him. One native gin only stated that she saw Mr. Wheeler, and when she was made to understand that he was said to have been holding the horses of the Native Police while they entered the scrub, she grew very angry, and was anxious to explain that he was sitting upon his own horse, with a pistol in his hand, at the edge of the scrub; she was exceedingly careful in making this clearly understood.

49. Then, would you admit the testimony of blacks as evidence against Europeans where life is concerned? I think it ought to be given and to be taken for what it is worth — it should be left to the jury to determine the value of the evidence. I may perhaps mention another instance to prove that the statements of the natives may be depended upon. When I went up to Fassifern, I called at a blacks' camp to make enquiries, and I was told by a Native in the camp where the bodies were; he said, amongst other things that he had thrown a red blanket over one of them, and that he was afraid to stop to bury him, for fear of being shot himself. Afterwards, when the bodies were discovered, I saw this black with the red blanket, and when the evidence was given, the body was clearly identified, and it was proved that he had no blanket on when he was shot. Other instances might be cited to prove the credibility of the blacks' evidence. With regard to the pistol, in corroboration of the gin's statement, it will be seen, that when Mr. Wheeler dismounted at Fassifern, he had a pistol in his hand — Mr. Hardie does not recollect the pistol, though he does not deny the statement; but Farringdon distinctly swears to the pistol.

FRIDAY 17 MAY 1861

Mr Henry Babbitt

1. By the Chairman: I believe you have been travelling through this Colony for some months? Yes, for 14 or 15 months.

2. Throughout the interior . . .? Yes. I wish to state that I do not come here as a voluntary witness, and that I have no complaint to make in giving my evidence.

3. . . . I believe you have been travelling in the neighbourhood of Rockhampton? Yes.
4. Will you state what occurred in that case in which you were concerned in connection with the Native Police — where did you meet them? Near a station called Calliangal, in the Dawson District.
5. Were the Native Police, when you came across them, in search of a prisoner? Yes.
6. Did you see that prisoner? I did.
7. Was he a white man or a black? He was a blackfellow.
8. Do you know his name? He was called Gulliver.
9. Do you know what was the nature of the crime for which he was supposed to have been taken? Yes. It was the murder of a woman at Rockhampton.
10. For the murder of Fanny Briggs? Yes.
11. Where did you see him? I first saw him on the banks of the Dee.
12. What was he doing? He was in custody of a party of draymen — they had secured him.
13. Where did you see him next? After I had been there half-an-hour, or perhaps an hour, the Native Police came up; they had been in pursuit of him for some time, and the draymen had captured him. The Native Police then put him into the carriage that I was travelling with. He had been intoxicated by the draymen when they took him, and quite stupified with liquor. He was bound hand and foot.
14. How was he bound? His arms were fastened behind him with a cord, and the same cord was fastened round his legs, which were drawn up so as to form a sort of triangle. That was done by the draymen. When he was put into the carriage his legs were unfastened, but his arms were still bound. The party then formed a guard round the prisoner. There were two or three white men from the Calliangal Station, and the Native Police and their officers, Lieut. Powell and Cadet Genetas — quite a formidable party altogether. They formed a guard behind, and a guard in advance, and one of them was in the carriage with the prisoner. We then drove about four miles to a scrub. The station we started from lies about three miles off the main road, and when we got to the junction of the main road with the station road, they took Gulliver out of the carriage and put him under a tree.
15. Who put him under the tree? The police.
16. Did any one order them to do so? The officers of the police put him there themselves; I dare say the troopers assisted them. He was thoroughly stupified with drink. The party belonging to the station then drove up with me to the Calliangal Station, from

which we had started in the morning. We started in order to bring Gulliver to the station, and met the Native Police on our way.

17. What became of Gulliver after that? I knew nothing further until a few minutes afterwards the Native Police arrived at the station without their prisoner. When they took him out of the carriage they said they were going to make him walk. They might have had the use of my carriage as far as the station, if they had wished. I think one of the Native Police came up first, and my impression was that he had merely come up for supplies, or something of the sort. I asked him what they were going to do with Gulliver, and he said, "He no keep away any more." Very soon afterwards the rest of the party came up. Some time after that, when I thought the police would be in a hurry to return to the place — where, as I supposed they had left Gulliver tied to a tree — as there appeared to me to be something singular about the affair, I asked one of the white men what had been done with Gulliver, and he said it was one of those things which ought not to be talked about.

18. Did you afterwards ascertain the fact — whether Gulliver had been disposed of or not? I said nothing further about it, but I knew from that, that he had been killed. I did not ascertain anything further. It was such a short time from my arrival at the station until the Native Police came up, that there was not time for Gulliver to have come to himself and to have made any attempt to escape.

19. Why did the Police not take him on in your carriage? They did not give me any reason.

20. Have you anything else to state? No. A long time after that I saw a printed report of the affair, and of Gulliver's being shot, the particulars of which seemed so different from my impressions on the subject, that I mentioned the fact to one or two persons, and I did not think any further notice would have been taken of it.

27. Were you not aware, by the published report from the Police to the Government, that Gulliver was shot while making his escape? I saw that report.

28. You stated that Gulliver, when you saw him, was in a helpless state of intoxication? Yes.

29. Could he not have recovered sufficiently to make his escape? I do not think so.

30. Do you not think the Native Police, seeing him in that state, might have been off their guard? I don't think it was possible for him to have escaped, he appeared so perfectly helpless.

31. Are you aware that there was a warrant out against Gulliver? I had heard there was.
32. Are you aware that when a warrant is out against a person, and he attempts to escape, it is justifiable to shoot him? Yes.
33. By Mr. Blakeney: You say that when you first saw Gulliver with the bullock-drivers he was tied hand and foot, and that the Police unfastened his legs when they put him into your vehicle? Yes.
34. When he was laid down at the foot of the vehicle only his arms or hands were tied? His arms were tied behind him.
35. And his feet were not tied? I think not.
36. Then an active blackfellow, with only his hands tied, could easily have made his escape? I think not; his arms were bound in a peculiar way, and he was in a very helpless condition. His whole system, when he was taken from the carriage, was like a loose rag.
37. Might he not have been feigning? It is possible, but I do not think so.

44. [By Mr. Fitzsimmons] Now, will you tell this Committee what reason you have for supposing that this man was shot? I have no other reasons beyond those I have stated.
45. Will you state the reasons which led you to that conclusion? Well, when I left him, Gulliver was a prisoner in the custody of the Native Police, and it was only a few minutes after that that the whole party came up to the station without their prisoner; and the next morning they went away by another road: they did not return to the same place at all. They remained at the station all that day, and went off the next morning in a different direction.
46. What time elapsed after you left Gulliver with the Native Police until their arrival at the station? Only a few minutes, it might have been half an hour or an hour, but it only appeared to me to be a very few minutes.
47. Will you answer what I asked you directly, instead of waiving the question by explanations, what was your reason for concluding that Gulliver had been shot? I have given you my reasons; there did not appear to me to have been time for him to have recovered and make his escape; and the blackfellow told me "that he wouldn't get away again;" and then the police did not return to the place again, for I saw their tracks, and know that they went a different way.

WEDNESDAY 22 MAY 1861

The Hon. Alfred William Compigné, MLC

1. By the Chairman: I believe you are a squatter in the Logan district? Yes.
2. Were not the blacks very troublesome in your district about the end of December last? Yes.

32. Have any of their hunting-grounds been taken away? No; they live chiefly on fish.
33. By Mr. Blakeney: Then they do not commit depredations from want of food? No, they are always very fat — at least all that I have seen have been so.
34. Was the damage to your property from the blacks considerable during the last year? No, the loss was not very great.

112. [By the Chairman] Now, with regard to the taking away gins by the Police, do you think that — constituted as the Native Police Force is at present — there are any means of preventing this? No, they are sure to take gins occasionally.
113. When a military force enters an enemy's country, is there not always great difficulty in preventing them from taking the females? Yes.
114. I wish to ascertain whether you think it possible to prevent the native troopers from taking gins, by any order given to the Force? The officers might do it to a certain extent, but not wholly.
115. Do you think the practice of taking gins by the troopers has a tendency to increase the number of outrages against the whites? Yes, to a certain extent, for, of course, it annoys the blacks.
116. You think, then, the practice ought to be prevented, if possible? Yes, it is the duty of every officer to do so, if possible.

124. Now, with regard to this outrage on the Logan, you stated — and it was also stated in Mr. Wheeler's evidence — that several tribes were present. Do you think they should all be treated as equal participators in the outrage, when the Police came upon them? Certainly, all that were there.
125. Are you aware that Mr. Wheeler singled out one particular tribe, and did not interfere with the others? I don't imagine that he could do so.

23 MAY 1861

Mr Samuel Sneyd

1. By the Chairman: You were formerly, I believe, in the old Mounted Police of New South Wales? I was.
2. You were a volunteer from one of the regiments? From the 4th regiment.
3. How many years were you in the Police Force? For over seventeen years — seventeen years and seven months.
4. You reached the rank of sergeant in that Force? Yes.

36. Do you remember a circumstance that took place on the Namoi, some years ago, when a number of white men were hanged for killing blacks? Who gave the information of that massacre? I think a man of the name of Hobbs; he is now Chief Constable in Windsor.
37. Were you ever patrolling in the neighbourhood? I was.
38. Was it not the case that a number of whites — comrades of these men who were executed — had been murdered? It was reported that such was the case.
39. That a number of the comrades of these men had been murdered by the blacks, and that being left to protect themselves, the whites were goaded on to the massacre, and attacked the blacks and shot some of them? I heard that such was the case.
40. Who gave the information? I understood that Hobbs was the principal person.

43. Are you aware that they were convicted on circumstantial evidence? I believe they were.
44. What was the number? Seven.
45. And they were all strung up in one morning? Yes, I believe so.
46. Do you think that any Government would dare to do such a thing at the present day? I could not answer that.
47. They were all prisoners of the Crown at that time? Yes, I believe so.
48. Do you remember that this affair raised a great outcry at the time against the Government? Yes.
49. And the Judges? Principally against Mr. Plunkett, the Attorney-General.
50. Is it not the case that the blacks broke out upon the Namoi again, and that a large detachment of Police was sent down, after this judicial murder, for I can call it

nothing else? I believe so — I believe it was the Mounted Police that were sent down in pursuit of the blacks there.
51. What number of Police went out with Major Nunn? I think about twenty. Major Nunn was in command of the party, and Lieutenant Cobham was second in command.
52. Were you among the number? I was.
53. What occurred on that occasion? Some of the blacks were shot after one or two of our men had been wounded; the first assault was by the blacks.

57. Was it not the case that Major Nunn was tried by court-martial, and that an inquiry was held at Invermain? He was not tried by court-martial, but an inquiry was held before the Magistrates at Invermain.
58. An inquiry was instituted by Government? Yes, before the Magistrates at Invermain, that being the nearest Bench to where the affair had taken place. I think one of the Crown Solicitors was sent up to assist the Magistrates; I think it was Mr. Moore Dillon, if I recollect right. The case was heard and dismissed — there was no charge against Major Nunn.
59. No charge proved? No charge proved.

FRIDAY 14 JUNE 1861

Mr O. Daly

62. By Mr. Ferrett: Did you see either of those white men, that you saw at the fire, fire a shot? No; how could I see a man fire a shot in the dark?
63. You say you have been in these parts twenty years, and that you have been about the Colony a great deal — have you ever known the blacks do any damage? I have not seen them do it, but I have heard of it.
64. Of your own knowledge, have you not known of it? Not of my own knowledge.
65. Have you never known them to rob huts, steal sheep, or destroy or spear cattle? No.
66. Never? No.
67. How long have you been in the Colony? Twenty years.
68. Have you never been brought into collision with the blacks, from their depredations committed on the property of any other person? No, never.

TUESDAY 18 JUNE 1861

John Ker Wilson, Esq.

1. By the Chairman: I believe you are a squatter of some years' standing? About 20 years.
2. In what is now called Queensland? I was a great deal in New South Wales, and a great deal about the Macintyre in the very worst times; and also in Moreton Bay during the first settlement in 1842.

4. How long were you at Kilcoy? Three or four months.
5. How long had the station been formed then? It was not formed at all, we had just got the sheep on it.
6. Were the blacks troublesome? Yes, we had two men killed. I had some assigned servants with me, and one of them, as well as a hired servant, were murdered while I was there; but that was done without our knowing anything about it; I mean we never came in collision with the blacks.
7. During your residence there were any of the blacks poisoned, or reported to be poisoned? I heard something of that, but not until after we left. I first heard of it from Mr. Merewether; I travelled with him in the same steamer with Sir George Gipps. Mr. Merewether began talking with me about the blacks and gave me all the particulars. I had not the slightest idea before that such a thing had occurred at all, but it must have happened somewhere about the time I was there.
8. Do you remember hearing of anything of the sort while you were at the station? I remember the overseer saying to me one day, "don't you think it would be a good thing to give these fellows a dose?" Of course I expressed my abhorrence of the suggestion and no more was said about it. I never heard anything further on the subject.

12. Were the blacks very troublesome? Very much so.
13. Before the formation of the Native Police Force? Yes.

23. Did any change take place after the arrival of the Native Police Force? Some change took place after a few gentlemen had come up and settled on the river. At the time when the murders were the worst there were only stockmen there, and a great many of the difficulties which took place with the blacks were owing, in a great measure, to the stations being weakly manned, and from the fact that the men were generally frightened; now when these men — hut-keepers, and others about a station — get alarmed, they frequently shoot at a blackfellow, or quietly give him a dose of poison, and the blacks take revenge for it, not always by killing the same man, but by taking the life of some white men . . .

27. What is your opinion of the Force as a Police Force? I think it is an efficient Force.
28. What is your opinion of the officers of the Force? I think a great deal depends upon the First Lieutenant; he is an officer perhaps quite as important to the efficiency of the Force as the Commandant — his local importance is greater — because on his conduct the acts of the junior officers in a great measure depend. But I think there is a fundamental error in the constitution of the Force.

37. What is the fundamental error in the Force to which you allude? Well, there is always a difficulty in reference to the legality of their proceedings from the fact of its being a Police Force, and it not being lawful for them to shoot the blacks.
38. Have you ever been out with the Native Police when they have come into collision with the blacks? Yes, upon one occasion, or rather the Police came towards me, it was a chance meeting. I have never been out with them myself.
39. Were you with them when they came into collision with the blacks? Yes, once.
40. Were the troopers sufficiently under the control of their officers? Oh, yes.
41. As much so as white men would be? I cannot say, but I think the system works badly, because some of the settlers require as much control as the Police. In every district there are always certain individuals who are more or less devoid of brains and common sense, who are at one time over indulgent to the blacks, and at another time will shoot them. A great deal of mischief arises from their treatment of the blacks, and much damage results from it. If the magistrates are obliged to overlook the doings of the Police, they must also overlook any imprudent acts committed by the settlers. The system does not appear to me to be a legal one and it would be impossible to pass any law to legalize the acts of the Force, because you would have to pass a law to render killing no murder. But if a Military Force were established instead of the Native Police, then any district requiring their services could be declared in a state of siege. The acts of the Force would then be legal, and the magistrates could act with them; besides which, the Government would be relieved from a great deal of embarrassment.

43. Are not the reports of disturbances with the blacks generally exaggerated? Yes, I know they are; there are always a number of persons up the country who go about from house to house — who, in fact, live by sponging upon the settlers — who tell and invent the most dreadful stories about the blacks and the Native Police to amuse their hearers, their sole object being to be asked to sit down and have their dinners. Many reports arise in this way which have no real foundation. I have heard many stories about white travellers being killed, and of outrages of different kinds; they do not perhaps the most of them reach this length, but they are very common up the country, and the further you go into the interior, the more numerous they are; that is the way they are raised.

58. By Mr. Blakeney: How long is it since there was a collision between the Police and the blacks in your district — a serious collision? The most serious one occurred last year; there was one trifling affair since then, but that was of no consequence. On the occasion I refer to there was a band of blackfellows headed by a fellow named "Bilba," who belonged to the tribe of Hornet Bank murderers; about thirty of these blacks kept together and lived in the mountains at the head of the Dawson. That band sometimes came down upon the stations, attacked them, and destroyed the cattle. Last year Mr. Coxen had formed a new station, and the quiet blacks about the place told him that Bilba's party were about to attack him. His people were greatly alarmed, and one of them went off for the police. Well, the blacks did come, and made every show of attacking the station; the Police arrived just as they had surrounded the place, and the blacks turned round and attacked the troopers; in fact, they showed fight, and sent a shower of spears at the white men. The country being very boggy just then, so that the horses were of no use, and the Police being suddenly attacked, the men dismounted, and a regular fight ensued, in which eighteen of the blacks were shot.

61. Were any of the officers or troopers wounded upon that occasion? I think one of the officers received a slight wound.

62. Was it Lieutenant Wheeler? No, I think it was Mr. Carr, the second lieutenant.

83. [By Mr. Watts] Now, in the course of your travels in the bush, have you observed whether the settlers, generally speaking, are kind or otherwise to the natives. I think the great mass of them are.

84. There are instances of cruelty here and there? Yes, and those instances generally occur through fear of the blacks. The system is going down now a good deal, though it is still in existence on the Balonne; I mean the system of keeping a single hutkeeper — generally an old prisoner — at a station, which is, perhaps, in an isolated position; those men are usually bad characters and they live in fear of their lives, and, actuated by their fears, they will occasionally fire at the blacks. There are commonly a number of bad characters who have escaped from the Police, or are afraid of meeting with them, about those stations, and it is those sort of men who do the mischief.

85. Do you know anything about the charges brought against the Native Police in the newspapers? No.

86. Is it not generally uneducated men, and not gentlemen, who commit these outrages on the blacks? Yes.

87. You have stated that it is through fear that many of the cruelties are perpetrated upon the blacks, which appears to me to be rather inconsistent — will you explain your meaning more clearly? Yes. I have known in former times, on the Macintyre, where two or three men might be living at a station together, who would employ the blacks and give them rations and tobacco; well, these men would be frightened out of their lives by the blacks and not being strong enough to go out and fight them, and living always in a state of fear, they would pop a gun through the slabs of the hut and fire upon them, and perhaps kill a blackfellow; at other times they would put poison in a damper and give it to the blacks. It was never the case when the stations were strongly manned, and, therefore, as I said before, fear of the blacks was the chief cause of these murders.

THURSDAY 20 JUNE 1861

John Hardie, Esq.

1. By the Chairman: I believe you are a squatter, living at Fassifern? Yes.

2. About the end of last year, or the beginning of the present year, were not the blacks very troublesome in your neighbourhood? Yes, very.

3. Spearing the cattle and robbing huts? Yes.

4. Did you communicate with Lieutenant Wheeler on the subject by sending him a letter? Yes.

5. And you requested him to come to your station and disperse the blacks? Yes.

10. Did Mr. Wheeler when he came to your station communicate with you at once? Yes, he came up and stopped with me that night.

11. And what did he do the next day? The next day he went to Coochin.

12. Did he disperse any of the blacks on your station? No, I don't think he did.
13. I suppose you are aware that one or two of them were killed there? I heard that one or two of them were dead, but I don't know how they were killed.
14. They were found dead — who found them? Some of the men on the station.
15. I suppose you heard it reported that some blacks had been shot? Yes.
16. But you are not aware, from your own knowledge, that Lieutenant Wheeler went out and killed any blacks on your run? No, I merely heard people say so.
17. Where were the bodies found? Within a paddock about a quarter of a mile, or perhaps a little more, from the station.
18. I presume you are aware that information was sent to the Coroner of the district, Dr. Challinor, to the effect that some blacks had been found dead? Who sent the information? I am not aware that it was sent.
19. Do you not know that Dr. Challinor came up and held an inquest on the bodies? I believe he did, but I was not at home at the time.
20. Did not you give evidence before him? Yes, at Ipswich.
21. Oh yes, it was at Ipswich — you gave evidence on oath? Yes, on oath.
22. Are you aware that Dr. Challinor wrote to the Attorney-General impugning your evidence, and charging you with falsehood? Did you take any notice of that? I did not.

---

25. Dr. Challinor says, "The story about a rape committed by two blackfellows on the daughter of one of the shepherds, eight months ago, may or may not be true, but after the false statements he made respecting the shooting of the aboriginals on the 24th December last, I should hesitate to believe it on his testimony alone." Was that evidence given on oath? I am sure I cannot say where he got it from.
26. You have stated to the Committee that you were not cognizant of anything further than the fact that there were some dead blacks found on your run, and that you wrote to Lieutenant Wheeler, requesting him to come to your station. Do you know anything more about it? No, I merely know that the blacks were dead, and it was said by some persons that they had been shot. I do not know that they were.

27. Did you hear any shooting near your station or on your run? I heard some shooting, but we had a man out shooting game. I cannot say that any blacks were shot.
28. Did not Lieutenant Wheeler leave your station with the intention of dispersing the blacks? I did not see him that day. I saw him the evening before.
29. Did not he tell you he would shoot them? No, he said he would disperse them.
30. Did you see any of the bodies? I saw one body.
31. Was death in that case by a gunshot wound? It looked more like a wound from a waddy. There had been several tribes of blacks about there lately, and several fights had taken place, and a blackfellow might have been killed in one of them by a blow from a waddy.
32. Did you recognise that blackfellow? No, I didn't know him by name.
33. Was he a young or an old man? An oldish man.
34. Had he white hair? His hair was a little grey.

48. By Mr. Blakeney: Was it not upon Christmas Eve that Lieutenant Wheeler came to your station? It was about mid-day, just before luncheon time.
49. What time did you say you saw him on that day? I saw him shortly after he arrived.
50. Was it before he arrived at your station that he dispersed the blacks? I believe so.
51. Then whatever was done was done before you saw him? I believe so.
52. Now recollect Mr. Hardie: Did Lieutenant Wheeler tell you that he had dispersed the blacks? — because there has been evidence to show that he had some conversation with you. Well, I think he told me that he had dispersed some blacks.
53. Is not the common acceptation of the term "dispersing" in reference to the blacks, "firing at them?" Well, you may disperse them without firing at them.
54. Yes, but is not that the general acceptation of the word? I believe it is.
55. Was it about a year-and-a-half before Christmas that this girl was violated? I think it was about that time.

62. What were the circumstances that came to your knowledge? I believe the blackfellow went to the sheep station where the girl was living, and told her she was wanted at the head station, and then, having enticed her out, knocked her down on the road.

63. Was he a blackfellow belonging to the neighbourhood? Yes, he is there now, going about Dugandan: I know him well enough.

72. By Mr. Moffitt: Do you recommend that any steps be taken about it? Yes; I should recommend that the Native Police should keep a look out, and, the first time they see him, shoot him.

John Mortimer, Esq.

1. By the Chairman: You reside in the Burnett District? Yes.
2. At a station called — ? Manumbar.
3. Is that near Toomcul? Yes; I am proprietor of Toomcul also, but I reside at Manumbar.
4. I believe you have a brother residing with you? Yes.
5. If I mistake not you were the author of a letter or communication to the COURIER about three months ago, relative to the death of some blacks? Yes.
6. And that letter contained charges against the Native Police Force? I put in an advertisement some time ago on the subject you refer to.
7. If you have any complaints to make, how was it that you did not make them direct to the Government, instead of adopting the unusual course of publishing them in an advertisement? I had several reasons.
8. Will you explain your reasons? One reason was that I thought my object would be accomplished without writing direct to the Government, and I thought I should prevent similar outrages being committed in future without any further trouble to myself, and without taking up the time of the Government. I did not think it necessary to write to the Government about it.
9. You received a communication from the Government shortly afterwards? Yes, I have it with me [*See Appendix A.*]
10. Did you answer it? I have a duplicate of my reply, which I can produce [*see Appendix B*]; it is a rough sketch, and perhaps there may be a few words altered, but the meaning is the same [*handing in both letters*].
11. Will you state some more of your reasons? I have stated my principal reason — that I did not wish to have any trouble about it myself, and I did not wish to put the Government to any trouble about it. I had seen Commissions appointed by the Government, the issue of which had been contrary to what I expected and I thought it might be the same thing in this case. I did not therefore think it necessary to notify the facts to the Government.

12. If I recollect right, the substance of your advertisement was an address to the Native Police Officers to the effect that if they chose to come and kill blacks up on your run, they should not leave them unburied? Yes, that was the substance of it.
13. Were you cognizant of outrages having been committed further than seeing the dead bodies of the blacks? Well, you will see if you read my correspondence. [*The Chairman here read the letters handed in by witness, referred to above.*]
14. I believe you have resided for some years in that part of the country? Yes.
15. Were the blacks very troublesome when you first went there? They had been troublesome a little before we went there, but they were not so troublesome when we first went up.
16. Did you ever apply for a detachment of Police to be stationed in your neighbourhood? Not to the best of my recollection, but after we had removed from Toomcul to our present station, and had been up there some years, we applied to the Police for assistance.
17. Did you not after that express to other persons besides the officer of the Police that you had been benefited by their protection? Not that I am aware of, either to the officer or to any one else.
18. Did your brother? My brother has only lately come to the Colony and knows nothing about it.
19. You have stated in this letter that a large gathering of the different tribes had taken place? Yes.
20. I suppose you have been long enough in the country to have seen the large assemblages of blacks in the Bunya season? Yes.
21. At that period they collect in large numbers and are usually very troublesome? My own opinion is that they are not more troublesome at those times; I was at first under the impression that they would be, but I have never found them so. It is perhaps necessary for the settlers to be a little more vigilant than at other times — that is all; the cattle will perhaps, get frightened, and run away from them.
22. That is your own experience, but do you know that they do not commit depredations at those times? I have enquired of some of my neighbours who live in Bunya districts, and of those who are most favourable to the Native Police, and they have attempted to evade the question; but, when I have put the question in this way, "If you were put upon your oath could you say you have had more trouble during the Bunya season than at other times?" they have been obliged to answer that they had not.

23. Had the blacks been committing depredations in your neighbourhood previous to this affair? I did not hear of any.
24. Did you hear that they had been giving trouble at Mr. Mackenzie's station, Collandale, and that they had threatened his wife and family? I never heard of that.
25. You are not aware then that any outrage had been committed by the blacks at that particular time? I did not hear of any, and I was not aware that any depredations had been committed.
26. Do you know a station called Imbil? Yes; I have never been to it, but it is near our station.
27. Have you heard of any depredations committed there lately? I have heard reports.
28. What were the reports? I heard from a young man residing at Yabber, who is down here now, that some blacks were shot at Imbil.
29. It has been broadly stated that upon this occasion some 30 or 40 natives were killed by the Police? I never stated that.
30. How many dead bodies did you see? I saw parts of four.
31. What was in your opinion the cause of death? I do not know.
32. You have stated in your letter that bullet wounds were the cause of death? Oh! I understood you to mean the cause of the outrage? There is no doubt about the cause of death in my opinion.
33. What reason have you for thinking so? Well, I judged from hearing the report of fire-arms, and from the appearance of the wounds. The rest of the people on the station heard the firing, and when I walked towards the place I met Lieutenant Morisset, about 300 yards from the camp.
34. Are you satisfied that they were gunshot wounds? I am satisfied in my own mind.
35. You have stated to the Committee that for anything you knew to the contrary, the blacks had committed no outrages — do you think it right that the Native Police should go and murder them in cold blood? Certainly not.
36. Have you heard any reports of such doings? I have read them in the papers.
37. Do you know where they came from — how they got into the Press? No.
38. You can speak from your own knowledge of the death of four blacks? Yes, but I am convinced there were many more.

39. What grounds have you for that belief? The blacks invited me to go and see the bodies, and although they frequently tell lies, they do sometimes tell the truth.
40. Why did you not go to see the bodies? Because I was satisfied with what I had already seen — or rather dissatisfied with it.
41. The Committee are extremely anxious to know the exact particulars in relation to this affair? Well, I will tell you what I saw, and the grounds upon which I believed that there were many more killed. The blacks, as I have stated, wished me to go and see the other bodies, but I would not go. They then told me that the Police, in riding along a bridle track from our station to Yabber, had met a blackfellow, and that they "had left him in the scrub;" that they met another black about five miles further, and "left him in the scrub." And further, Mr. Swanson informed me that, when they went to Yabber, on the way they apprehended two deserters from the Police, and that they camped there that night, the blacks being camped near the head station. When they saw the Police coming, some of Mr. Swanson's blacks came to the head station, and one of them left his blanket there; one of the Police took it, and the black came back and demanded it of him; the trooper would not give it up, and threatened to shoot the blackfellow, who then went to Mr. Swanson; Mr. Swanson went to Mr. Morisset, and identified the blanket and the man had to give it up. Well, the next day they went out on the run, Mr. Morisset and his troopers, and Mr. Swanson wanted to go with them, in order to stop them from shooting any of his blacks. He started with them, and took one of his own blacks with him, and after going over part of the run Mr. Swanson went home, and left the black to point out to the Police any of the quiet and peaceable blacks. Afterwards they came upon a camp of natives, and the Police fired upon the camp; some of the blacks ran away, and some stopped, and one fellow, who had been shepherding for Mr. Swanson, and for me also, was so confident of his safety that he would not run, and he stopped about the horses with Mr. Swanson's black. This man was singing out to the Police, "This fellow Mr. Swanson's blackfellow, baal shoot him," and he was shot at the tail of one of the horses. I have no doubt at all about that. Another blackfellow, I believe, was killed, and put into a hollow log. I believe those blacks were all shot, two between the stations, and four at our station which I saw myself.
42. As I understood you; Mr. Swanson was not present when the shooting took place? No.
43. Then this is merely evidence from the blacks themselves? From Mr. Swanson.

44. But you say he was not present? He was present when the Police had to give up the blanket.
45. You are aware that this is a very serious charge, and that it ought to rest upon substantial evidence. You have stated that the blackfellows tell the truth at times, and at other times they do not. Here is a statement that three or four blackfellows were murdered by the Police: now, do you think it right that any officer should be tried and convicted upon the evidence of those blackfellows? I think their evidence should not be admissible but we believe them just the same.

93. [By Mr. Watts] Do you think that, for merely spearing cattle, the lieutenant would be justified in shooting them in that way? I do not, unless it might be some notorious ringleader who was known all through the district; he might then be justified in shooting one of them, but not for an indiscriminate slaughter.
94. By the Chairman: Do you think it is the duty of this Committee — supposing he has committed the outrage — to recommend his dismissal? Yes.

101. Will you inform the Committee what is the name of the officer who was in charge on the occasion on which these outrages were committed? To the best of my knowledge it was Lieutenant Morisset.
102. Is he any relative of the Commandant? I cannot tell.

139. [By Mr. Blakeney] Did you hear that any cattle had been killed during that Bunya season — did you hear of any complaints from the squatters? No; I did not.
140. Did you hear it from any one else besides Lieutenant Morisset? No.

156. [By Mr. Moffatt] How long is it since you went there in the first place? About 10 years.
157. Did you suffer any outrages while there at the hands of the blacks? No.
158. Did they ever interfere with your stock? Not that I can recollect.
159. Did you have any men killed by them? No.
160. Then have you had any trouble with the blacks since you went to live at Manumbar? Yes.

WEDNESDAY 26 JUNE 1861

Thomas Petrie, Esq.

1. **By the Chairman: Are you a native of this district?** No.
2. **But you have been a number of years residing in it?** Yes.
3. **I believe you came to this country as a boy?** Yes; I was only three months old when I left home.
4. **I believe you can speak the language of the blacks?** Yes, just the same as they do themselves — that is to say, the blacks of this tribe.
5. **You have, of course, seen a great deal of the blacks?** Yes.
6. **Were you here at the time that the German Missionaries were at work among them?** Yes.
7. **From what you have heard from the blacks themselves, are you aware whether the missionaries met with any success in their efforts to Christianize or civilize them?** No, I do not think they did.
8. **Did you know the old Brisbane tribes?** Yes; they are nearly all dead now: there are only about five of them left.

17. **Do you know anything of the Native Police?** Yes. I was going to say that the bad conduct of the blacks is in a great measure the fault of the white people themselves, and the way in which they treat them. I have been living where no one else was able to remain, and I have had several hundreds of the blacks about me.
18. **What do you mean by their own fault?** They make promises to the blacks, and do not keep them.
19. **Have you ever heard any opinions of the Native Police from the blacks?** Yes; they do not like them at all: many of them were shot by the police.
20. **What were they shot for?** It was said they were shot for cattle stealing, but the blacks said that no cattle were stolen at that time.
21. **What detachment of police was concerned in that affair?** I think they were from Sandgate.

28. **What do you think of the plan proposed — that a party of missionaries should establish a cotton-growing plantation, on which the older natives should be kept at work, while the children were put to school and taken care of?** Yes, it might answer, if they were kept out of the town, and not allowed to go where they could get drink. There might be

some trouble with them for the first year, but those who came would tell the rest, and it might do some good.

29. I am speaking of it as an experiment? Yes, but the missionaries would have to be a little different from the last.

30. What was their fault? They did not teach the natives much: they kept them at work in their own gardens more than at anything else.

34. How long have you been here altogether? About 26 or 27 years.

35. I mean constantly in contact with the blacks? Yes, about that time, except occasionally for short periods.

45. Have you ever observed that they entertain any idea of religion or the existence of a Supreme Being? No; they do not believe that they die a natural death. If one of them dies, they believe that a blackfellow with a stone out of his belly has killed him beforehand, cut him into pieces, and put him together again. They used to believe that when they died they would "jump up whitefellows;" but they don't believe that so generally now.

46. What do you mean by cutting into pieces? That is their belief. If a blackfellow dies they believe he has been previously killed and cut up by some other blackfellow, and then when his death really takes place they attribute it to that cause.

47. Then they believe in two deaths? Yes.

48. By Mr. Blakeney: Whereabouts were those blacks shot about six or seven months ago? At Mr. Griffin's station, on the Pine River.

49. How many of them were killed? Five.

50. Was that done by Mr. Wheeler's detachment from Sandgate? I think the Police were from Sandgate: I am not acquainted with the officer, but I think that was his name.

59. Are there any white women at your station? Yes.

60. Do you consider them particularly safe there? Quite safe.

61. Why should they be more so there than in the vicinity of the town? I do not know, but I can trust the blacks with everything I have; they would not do me any injury, I have known them so long.

SATURDAY 6 JULY 1861

E.M.V. Morisset, Esq., Commandant of Native Police Force

1. By the Chairman: You are Commandant of the Native Police Force? Yes.

2. Have you not lately sent in your resignation (not yet accepted)? Yes.
3. What are your reasons for resigning? I have been obliged to reside at Rockhampton, and my wife's health will not allow of her remaining there.
4. You are aware that an enquiry has been instituted into the management of the Native Police Force, in consequences of charges having been made against the Force, of outrages committed by them in the performance of their duties? Yes.
5. Do you know anything of these charges? Most of the circumstances, on which the charges were founded, have been reported to me.
6. The officers have sent in reports? Yes; continually.
7. The first charge if I recollect right, was that of the misconduct of the Native Police, in the case of Fanny Briggs, at Rockhampton. I believe there is no doubt but that she was murdered by the troopers of the Native Police? I believe she was.

14. As to the cause of the murder — was she not in the habit of supplying the troopers with spirits, when they went to look after her horses? I believe that was the case: I have been told so, by Mr. Murray.
15. You don't know it of your own knowledge? No, excepting that I saw in a letter she once wrote to Mr. Watts that some of her mares had been lost, and that Toby was going out the next day after them, and that she had promised him a bottle of grog. The next she was murdered.
16. Toby was one of the troopers? Yes; one who was constantly there.
17. You saw the letter yourself? Yes, and several others saw it.

21. There was another man concerned in the affair — one Gulliver? He was shot by the Native Police.
22. Evidence has been given before the Committee, to the effect that he was captured by some bullock drivers, and handed over to the Native Police? Yes.
23. Was he shot in attempting to make his escape? So it was reported, and I believe the report was true.
24. Who was the officer in charge of him? Lieutenant Powell.
25. Did he report to you that Gulliver was well secured, and in a state of insensibility from drink, and put into a

person's carriage? He told me he had been carried, and bound hand and foot, but that he was only feigning intoxication.
26. And this took off the attention of the troopers, and he thus attempted to make his escape? The troopers had been sent away to procure rations, and Mr. Powell, and I think another officer and trooper, were left alone with Gulliver; he said the rope was cutting his feet, and they took it off; he then attempted to escape, and Lieutenant Powell, or the trooper with him, shot him.
27. Lieutenant Powell shot him himself? I am not sure whether it was Lieutenant Powell or one of the troopers.
28. Lieutenant Powell was present? Yes.
29. Where is Lieutenant Powell now? On the Burdekin.
30. The next charge brought against the Police is that of killing some old blacks and gins on the Logan and at Fassifern. What report was sent in to you by Lieutenant Wheeler, in reference to that? It was reported to me that the blacks had for some time been spearing cattle in that district, and Lieutenant Wheeler, in consequence, went to Mr. Compigné's Station, where he got on the tracks of the blacks, and followed them to the Dugandan scrub. They had been robbing huts as well as killing cattle.
31. Lieutenant Wheeler stated that when after the blacks, he came upon three or four tribes together, — that he divided these blacks, taking those he believed to have committed the depredations, and that he sent the troopers into the scrub, in the dark, and ordered them to fire on these blacks, and that a gin was killed. Do you not consider that exceeding his instructions? Do you think that a proper way of acting? No; if that is exactly what he did, he certainly did exceed his instructions; it is not part of his instructions to fire on the blacks without a cause.

[Numbers 30 to 39 are repeated in original transcript.]

30. Don't you consider he was rather indiscreet in the case referred to? Yes. I think so.
31. Have you ever taken him to task? I have never had occasion, except in this instance, at Fassifern.
32. But do you think in this instance he exceeded his instructions somewhat? I think he must have been rather indiscreet.
33. How long has he been in the Force? I think some four years; he has been on the Fitzroy, and at Port Curtis.
34. The next charge brought against the Native Police, is that of slaughtering a number of blacks unnecessarily

in the neighbourhood of Mr. Mortimer's Station, on the Burnett. Mr. Mortimer has been examined by the Committee, and also Mr. Parkinson, and certainly the Native Police do not come favourably out of the enquiry. It appears that Lieutenant Morisset, of the Native Police, was travelling up the country with horses. Had he any instructions to deviate from his route, and take charge of a detachment of Police? No instructions from me, but he received instructions to return back from Wide Bay, from Lieutenant Murray.

35. How long has Lieutenant Morisset been in the Force? Hardly twelve months, I think.

36. Do you not think it improper to entrust such a young officer with the charge of a detachment, in such a case as this? I don't think so, because, although Lieutenant Morisset had not been long in the Force, he had had as much experience with the Native Police Force as many of the officers.

37. Do you think Mr. Murray was justified in giving him charge of the detachment? I think Mr. Murray should have gone himself.

38. It appears from the evidence of Mr. Mortimer and another, that the detachment in charge of Lieutenant Morisset was sent up on the representations of Mr. Parkinson and some others, and that they killed a number of blacks, and left them lying dead about his run — we have heard of at least eight found dead in that way. Do you think this a justifiable act under the circumstances? Yes, I think so; perhaps I may be allowed to explain. I received a report from Mr. Morisset (*Vide appendix B*) which is now in the Colonial Secretary's office; he was on his way to head-quarters with a number of horses, and when he got to this district on his way up to Wide Bay, he was informed by several squatters that the blacks were very troublesome killing cattle, and that they threatened to attack the horses. He reported this to Mr. Murray, when he got to Wide Bay and Lieutenant Murray sent him back with a detachment of his own men. When Mr. Morisset got back, he found the blacks in large numbers at the Bunya Bunya, and, I think, he first dispersed them there, and then met them again somewhere else — at least, the blacks found he was following them, and went in towards the station of the Messrs. Mortimer, and got close to it, when the Police came up with them. I believe they thought the Police were coming to shoot them, and made the first attack. The report that has been sent in to the Colonial Secretary has not explained that as fully as I have done as I collected more particulars from my brother afterwards, having examined him when he came in to head-quarters.

39. Don't you think the report should have been as full a one as possible? It should; but it was written before I had seen my brother.

40. Was it not the duty of Lieutenant Murray to have reported? I received a report from Mr. Murray also.

44. How long has Mr. Murray been in that district? About six months.

45. Lieutenant Bligh was stationed there sometime? Yes.

46. Were the blacks tolerably quiet then? They have always been troublesome at the head of the Mary.

47. Is it a good plan to remove officers from a district when they get used to it? No; but in this case I was obliged to remove Lieutenant Bligh.

48. Why? Because I wanted him at head-quarters, where he was much more useful than at Wide Bay.

49. Have you had a report of the circumstances connected with the charge against the native Police, of killing the blacks unnecessarily at Maryborough? Yes; and it was forwarded by me to the Colonial Secretary.

50. Mr. Bligh can give us all the necessary information on that subject? Yes.

51. Are you aware that a great many letters have been put in the papers anonymously, in reference to these charges? Yes, a great many.

56. A great many letters have appeared in the newspapers signed — "One who knows too much of the Native Police" — have you any idea who wrote them? I might guess, but I could not tell with any certainty; I think the letter I have seen with that signature must have been written by Mr. Alfred Brown.

57. This letter enters very minutely into the management of the Native Police, and looks as if the writer had received his information from an officer of the Force — have you any suspicion who this might have been? Yes; I am certain that the information was derived from one of the officers, and the letter I allude to states that the officers at Port Curtis were served out with the worst pack-saddles and horses, and reflects generally on my management. I believe that the letter was written by Mr. Alfred Brown.

58. From whom do you suppose he got his information? From second Lieutenant Baker, Port Curtis.

72. Are you aware that many of the other officers are addicted to intemperance? I am not aware of many.
73. Are you aware of any? Yes.
74. As far as the evidence goes, it appears that the ineffectiveness of the Native Police Force is entirely owing to the inefficiency of the officers . . . How long has Lieutenant Murray been in the Force? About five years.
75. Do you consider him an efficient officer? He certainly has been till he gave way to habits of intemperance — none more so.
76. Have you seen him in a state of intoxication? Yes.
77. More than once? Yes.
78. How is it you never represented the matter to the Government, and recommended his dismissal? Because he always promised to reform; and another reason was, that I thought it a very delicate matter, having been appointed Commandant over his head.
79. Do you consider that any delicacy of feeling on your part should interfere with your duties as Commandant? I don't think it should have done.
80. Do you think it conduces to the efficiency of the Force that there should be officers in it addicted to these habits? Certainly not.
81. Don't you think that an officer addicted to these habits might be in a state of intoxication, when out patrolling, and might in that state come upon a tribe of blacks? No, I don't think it possible.
82. Why? They could not get grog in the interior.
83. Might they not get grog at the station they started from in the morning — don't you think it likely? I am sure that would not be the case with Mr. Murray.
84. There have been instances, to the knowledge of a Member of the Committee, in which this has been the case. The late Mr. Fulford and Mr. Irving have been known to be drunk at stations for days together? I did not know anything of Mr. Fulford; he died before I was made Commandant.
85. As it is your intention to leave the Force, can you conscientiously recommend that Mr. Murray should remain in it, supposing that the present Force is not disbanded? If he continues in habits of intemperance, he would be unfit to carry out his duties.
86. The next officer is Mr. John O'Connell Bligh — how long has he been in the Force? Nearly eight years.
87. Do you consider him an efficient officer? Yes.

88. Perfectly temperate? Most particularly so.
89. Energetic? Yes.
90. Altogether a good officer? Yes, I should say the best in the Force.

94. The next is Mr. Powell — how long has he been in the Force? I should think about five years.
95. What occupation did he follow before he went into the Force? He followed a great many; he was in Mexico, and also sometime in California, and for many years a sailor.
96. How did he get his appointment? He was recommended by Mr. Murray.
97. His appointment took place since you have been Commandant? No, before.
98. Do you consider him an efficient officer? He was for some time; but he has latterly been addicted to intemperate habits.

100. But to your certain knowledge, Mr. Powell is addicted to drink? Yes.
101. Also, if he was at one time energetic, he has become very much the reverse lately? He has certainly shown a great deal of inactivity lately.
102. Now, Mr. Morisset, seeing the great importance of an efficient Police Force to the new district of Kennedy, may I ask, should Mr. Powell have been sent there in charge of a detachment, chiefly of raw recruits? It was only when Mr. Powell got his promotion that I perceived he was unfit for the position; but the men sent up were not all raw recruits.

121. Next on the list is Mr. G.P.M. Murray — is he any relation to Mr. John Murray? Brother; he is a most efficient officer.
122. How long has he been in the Force? Nearly four years; he was appointed soon after Mr. Carr.

176. I have forgotten one of the officers — Lieutenant Morisset — what is your opinion as to his efficiency? I think him a very efficient officer; he has had a great deal of experience.
177. Do you think that he did not act with very great indiscretion in the affair at the Messrs Mortimer? I think not.
178. Do you think he had any business to deviate from the instructions given by the Commandant; and take charge of a detachment of Lieutenant Murray's? I think he could not help doing so in a case of emergency as that was: Lieuten-

ant Murray was his senior officer, and he could not well refuse to obey him.

179. I again ask — do you think that a young officer should be intrusted with a detachment and go blazing away into the blacks in that way? I don't know that he should go blazing away into the blacks, but his former experience was quite enough to entitle him to take charge of a detachment in any case.

APPENDIX B

Rockhampton, 10th April, 1861.

SIR, — I have the honor to inform you that I arrived here yesterday, with (32) thirty-two horses, the same having been purchased by me for the use of the Native Police.

On my way up from Brisbane I found it necessary to rest the horses for some time at Wide Bay, and in consequence of the numerous complaints sent in by the squatters, of the frequent and daring outrages of the blacks at the Bunya Bunya, I received instructions from Lieutenant Murray to patrol the district with a detachment of men. I found the blacks collected in several places in very large numbers, and also that they had been killing cattle at nearly all the stations in that district: and on two or three occasions I found it necessary to fire upon them before they would disperse.

At Messrs. Frazer and Parkinson's, and also at Mr. Lawless' cattle station, they were spearing cattle even while I was on the station.

I have the honor to enclose brands and descriptions of horses purchased by me.

I have, &c.,
(Signed) E.V. MORISSET,
Second Lieutenant Native Mounted Police

Native Police Force Chairman's Report

THE SELECT COMMITTEE of the Legislative Assembly, appointed by ballot on the 1st May, 1861, with power to send for persons and papers, and sit during any adjournment of the House, to enquire into and report on the organisation and management of the Native Police Force; and further to enquire into and report how far it may be practicable to ameliorate the present condition of the aborigines of this Colony, have agreed to the following Report:—

Your Committee, entering on their duties fully impressed with the importance of the subjects under consideration, have examined upwards of thirty witnesses, including the principal Officers of the Native Police Corps, and have thus collected a mass of evidence of the most comprehensive character.

To make this record more complete, your Committee have availed themselves of portions of the evidence taken before a Select Committee held in Sydney in the year 1858, and in addition, the Appendices attached to this Report contain much valuable information.

Your Committee cannot but express their regret that more than one witness, capable of affording important information regarding the Native Police, should have refused to submit themselves to an examination.

The questions brought under the notice of your Committee have been:—

1. The present condition and organization of the Native Police Force.
2. The charges of unnecessary cruelty brought against their officers when dealing with the Natives, and protecting the settlers against their aggressions.
3. The prospect of civilising, or in any way improving the condition of the aboriginal population.

I. In acquiring information on the subject of the working of the Native Police, your Committee, by selecting persons from all classes, have endeavoured to avoid making the evidence merely the expression of the views of any section of the community, favourable or otherwise, to the abstract question of the employment of an aboriginal protective Force.

The whole weight of the evidence, with one or two exceptions, tends to prove:—

1. That any change in the organisation of this Force by the substitution of white troopers for Native, would destroy its efficiency.
2. That since its establishment and reconstruction under its present Commandant, the destruction of property and loss of life on either side has considerably diminished.
3. That any attempt to disband the Force suddenly, would, as on a previous occasion, lead to disastrous results.

It is clearly shown by the evidence of the Commandant and some of the witnesses, that any want of discipline that has existed in this Force, or any excesses that are attributable to the Troopers, have arisen mainly from the inefficiency, the indiscretion, and the intemperate habits of some of the Officers, rather than from any defect in the system itself.

It also appears evident that no advantage would accrue on the score of economy, by a re-construction of this corps in the way that has been proposed by some of the witnesses. Your Committee, therefore, have directed their attention to the necessity of improving the internal organisation of the existing Native Police, and, in pursuing this enquiry, the following points have presented themselves as worthy of recommendation:—

1. That it is of the highest importance to secure the services of efficient Officers; the successful working of the Force depending almost entirely on their energy, ability, and sobriety. That Cadets should be appointed, who should serve a certain period under the supervision of the head of the Force before they are considered eligible to hold commissions, and that appointments to the Corps should be made solely on the recommendation of the Commandant for the time being, who should be held responsible for the efficiency of his Officers.
2. That no detachment of Native Police should be stationed in the vicinity of any of the towns, as the facilities for obtaining intoxicating liquors tend to demoralize the Troopers, and have, in some cases, resulted in the most serious outrages and breaches of the law.
3. That the Troopers should, in all cases, be recruited from districts at a distance from those in which they are likely to be employed.
4. Monthly returns of all proceedings, and the state of the troops, should be forwarded by each Officer in command of a detachment to the Commandant of the Force, who would furnish a general abstract thereof to the Colonial Secretary, or the head of the Executive Department, under which he may be placed.
5. A more simple and efficient system of keeping the accounts, and furnishing the supplies of clothing, ammunition, &c., to the different divisions, appears to your Committee highly necessary, and, unless in cases where it may be urgently required, your Committee deprecate the practice of removing efficient Officers from the districts they have been accustomed to serve in.

II. The charges brought against the Officers of the Native Police have been investigated as far as practicable.

Your Committee, although aware how difficult it may be in cases where depredations are committed by the blacks to make them amenable to British Law, cannot countenance the indiscriminate slaughter which appears on more than one occasion to have taken place.

Lieutenant Wheeler appears to have acted with indiscretion on his late visit to the Logan and Fassifern. Your Committee recommend that he should be reprimanded, and removed to another district: were it not that in other respects he is a most valuable and zealous Officer, they would feel it their duty to recommend his dismissal.

With respect to the affray at Mr. Mortimer's, it appears that the detachment of Police stationed at Maryborough was most improperly handed over by the Officer in charge, Lieutenant Murray, to Second Lieutenant Morrisset, a young officer newly appointed, unacquainted with his duties, and also with the Troopers placed under his control. It also appears by the evidence that the natives had been committing depredations in that neighbourhood for some time previous, and that the assistance of the Police had been demanded. It is likewise shown by Mr. Morrisset's report that they attacked the Police in the first instance. After a careful consideration of the evidence in this case, your Committee recommend that Lieutenant Murray should be removed from the Force, both on this account, and his general unfitness for his duties.

Lieutenant Bligh appears, as far as evidence in his case was procurable, to have been justified in his attack on the natives in the town of Maryborough. He is generally spoken of as a zealous and efficient officer, and bears a high character from the Commandant.

Your Committee having been informed that the present Commandant has resigned, or is about to resign, his appointment, feel themselves relieved from the necessity of making any comments on his management of the Force.

Touching the murder of Fanny Briggs by Troopers of the Native Police, it does not appear to your Committee that this unfortunate occurrence militates in any way against the Force. The detachment was stationed too near the Town of Rockhampton, which gave facilities for procuring liquor. The Troopers were on friendly terms with this young woman, and, by the evidence of the Commandant, Mr. Morrisset, it will be seen that she promised Toby, one of the Troopers, a bottle of grog if he found the horses belonging to the station. On the day after this note was written she was murdered. Instances of rape and murder resulting from the influence of liquor, have occurred when the aborigines committing such excesses have not been members of the Police Force.

III. The evidence taken by your Committee shews beyond doubt, that all attempts to Christianize or educate the aborigines of Australia have hitherto proved abortive. Except in one or two isolated cases, after being brought up and educated for a certain period, the Natives of both sexes invariably return to their savage habits. Credible witnesses shew that they are addicted to cannibalism; that they have no idea of a future state; and are sunk in the lowest depths of barbarism. Missions have been established amongst them at different periods with but partial success; and the same may be said of the schools established in the different Colonies.

Nevertheless, any improvement in the social condition of this benighted race is an object so desirable of attainment, that your Committee feel justified in recommending to the notice of the Government the plan sketched forth in the evidence of Mr. Zillman, whose great experience entitles his opinion to favourable consideration.

This proposal embraces the establishment of a Missionary Cotton Company, who, receiving land and other assistance from the Government, would endeavour to educate the children while employing the parents in the necessary work of the plantation. Such a proposal appears to your Committee sufficiently feasible to justify a trial. Should it succeed, the system may be operated upon to any extent.

In bringing their labours to a close, your Committee are desirous to bring under the notice of your Honourable House the assistance they have received from several of the witnesses, who, at great personal inconvenience to themselves, have given so much valuable information.

R.R. MACKENZIE, CHAIRMAN.

Author's Comments on the Select Committee's Enquiry

So, there it is — the great Senate enquiry into the Native Police Force. It went absolutely nowhere except, perhaps, to illuminate the point that, so long as Justice was seen to be done, the Government of 1861 cared nothing for the Aborigines!

The newspapers lampooned the Government debate on the Report mercilessly, as seen in the *Courier*, Saturday 27 July 1861:

> Before entering with that minuteness which the matter demands upon the consideration of the Report of the Select Committee on the Native

Police, and of the evidence accompanying that document, it is necessary to recur to the debate, or discussion — for debate it can scarcely be called — which has taken place on the subject. The very singular speech with which the Colonial Treasurer Mr R.R. Mackenzie, the enquiry chairman, who later became Premier, brought forward the report on Wednesday evening was more than paralleled in inconsecutiveness and folly by Mr MACALISTER'S display on Thursday afternoon; and the horrors of Mr Watts were scarcely so gloomy as the confessions of Mr GORE; but they all went in great measure astray from the subject. They fell with great vehemence on the character of the unhappy Aborigines, but the efficacy or inefficacy of any measures hitherto adopted for their reclamation, or the causes of their failure, were apparently of very slight weight on their minds . . . Mr MACALISTER, indeed, made a furious onslaught on the unhappy Aborigines. They had no idea of a future state — they were cannibals — they were murderers — they were ravishers — they were even (horrible fact!) cattle stealers . . . But Mr MACALISTER, while dwelling on and deploring the outrages, or rather stated outrages, for they were not proved — they were matters for the most part of hearsay — by the Aborigines on female residents upon stations, totally forgot the prevalent and far more atrocious violence so frequently offered to the gins.

Newspaper articles, letters to the Editor, editorials — they went on for ages. One man even wrote:

> God, to whom innocent blood cries from the ground now, as it did when Abel was murdered, — who knows no distinction of white and black in this matter . . .

I would like to include a letter — in part — written to the Secretary of the Board of National Education, Sydney. It was written by Mr W.A. Duncan, JP.

> There is, I am convinced, no human power of civilizing or even of perpetuating the race, who, while they are rapidly disappearing by disease and other causes, receive but little increase in the natural way, in consequence of the promiscuous intercourse of their women with the white man.

"Promiscuous intercourse of their women with the white man!" What a misleading phrase. It appears to me that Mr Duncan was in error with the gender. I will leave Mr Duncan's sophism for the reader to judge.

Finally, I feel obliged to mention one other scheme that was mooted during the 1860s; it was the proposal by various people — mainly missionaries — to establish a cotton-growing industry; this enterprise was to be manned with Aboriginal labour. Another Deep South?

Notes

Introduction

1. Editorial. *Northern Argus*, Rockhampton, 1864.
2. R.H. Mathews, *The Wombya Organization of the Australian Aborigines,* p.390.
3. Minutes of Evidence: Select Committee on the Queensland Native Police Force, 1861, pp.18–19. Author's italics.
4. Bill Rosser, *Dreamtime Nightmares,* AIAS, Canberra, 1985.
5. Ibid.
6. See notes 45, 47, 52, 71 in notes to main text.
7. Letter of Dismissal, 19 January 1855. (NSWVP)
8. Registrar of Births, Deaths and Marriages, Brisbane.
9. *Sunday Mail*, 10 January 1988.
10. Constance Petrie, *Tom Petrie's Reminiscences of Early Queensland,* Brisbane, 1907, p.18.
11. Ibid., pp.33–34.
12. E.B. Kennedy, *The Black Police of Queensland,* London, 1902.
13. Letter from Wickham to Colonial Secretary, 10 January 1859. Author's italics.
14. Letter from Wheeler to Wickham, 5 March 1859.
15. Edric Norfolk Vaux Morisset was the son of the Superintendent of the Macquarie convict settlement. On 14 February 1853, he was appointed Lieutenant in the Native Police Force. He was appointed because of his knowledge of bushcraft and his understanding of the ways of the Aborigine. He tendered his resignation immediately prior to the opening of the Select Committee's enquiry in 1861.
16. Bill R. Thorpe, Report to Select Committee on the Aborigines, SAPP, 1897, pp.113–17.
17. QVP, 1861, p.572.

18. Henry Reynolds, *Frontier*, Allen and Unwin, Sydney, 1987.
19. *Courier*, 30 May 1861.
20. Minutes of Evidence: 1861 Select Committee, p.48. Author's italics.
21. Ibid. p.137. Author's italics.
22. Ibid. p.147. Author's italics.
23. Ibid. pp.143–44. Author's italics.
24. Ibid. p.152.
25. Ibid. p.138. Author's italics.
26. Select Committee on the Native Police Force, *Report* 1861, pp.3–4. Author's italics.

"They used to flog me with a whip"

1. Bill Rosser, *Dreamtime Nightmares*.
2. A bob was a shilling.
3. Queensland Aboriginal Act (repealed 1984).
4. Under the Regulations of the Queensland Aboriginal Act, an Aborigine could be — and was — forced to work on cattle stations for a period of twelve months. Permission from the Queensland Department of Aboriginal Affairs was not required as the necessary clause was written into the Act. Many retired stockmen to whom I have spoken have told me that they were simply picked up off the streets of country towns and spirited away to a station (see *Dreamtime Nightmares*).
5. The biography of Jack Punch is included in *Dreamtime Nightmares*. This most absorbing story tells of Jack's tribal customs, his culture and his experiences as a stockman on cattle stations.

"Lost 'em shoein' 'orses"

6. See *Dreamtime Nightmares*.
7. Ruby DeSatge drove out to the bush daily to shoot a kangaroo or two with which to feed Dajarra's hungry dogs. Of course, the meaty rumps and the tails were kept for the consumption of some of the town's inhabitants.

"Only tents and bough sheds"

8. Lake Nash is a cattle station located north-west of Urandangie. It is possibly the only district left in Queensland where Aborigines still practise genuine customs and culture.
9. Both are cattle stations in Western Queensland.

"A lot were lying around . . . shot"

10. The Kalkadoon tribe, which occupied a large area in the Mt Isa district, was considered to be perhaps the most fierce and warlike in Queensland and, possibly, in Australia.
11. Norman Tindale's *Tribal Boundaries in Aboriginal Australia* shows that Telemon Station fell within the tribal boundary of the Jukambe tribe. As there is no "Telemon" tribe shown, it is most probable that, as Cyclone Jack suggested, the Telemons took their name from the station around which they lived. Telemon Station was situated near the headwaters of the Logan River.
12. *Rockhampton Bulletin*, 18 June 1867. Author's italics.

"Had my countenance betrayed me?"

13. Minutes of Evidence: 1861 Select Committee, p.3.

"Kill the bastards!"

14. Minutes of Evidence: 1861 Select Committee, p.16. Wheeler received no such letter. He stated in his report to the Colonial Secretary, dated 1 January 1861 (para. 3), that he had seen "a letter from Mr Hardie of Fassifern, stating that a large mob of blacks were killing his cattle", (Wheeler/Col. Sec.—61/1.J. QSA). This letter was disputed (*Moreton Bay Courier*, 14 February 1861). However, on 25 March 1861 he again wrote, saying the letter was now in the possession of the Col. Sec. There is no record as to when or how it came into the possession of the Col. Sec. The *Moreton Bay Courier* pointed out, "In his evidence before the Magistrate [Henry Challinor, at

Ipswich], Mr Hardie says nothing of having written such a letter."

15. Arthur W. Jose, *History of Australia*, Angus & Robertson, Sydney, 1911, 4th edition.
16. Minutes of Evidence: 1861 Select Committee, pp.18–19.
17. Wheeler was charged with murder in the Rockhampton Circuit Court in 1876. He was charged with the brutal murder of an Aboriginal youth. It was claimed that he had tied the lad to a verandah rail and whipped him until the whip broke. He then continued the flogging using the girth strap of a saddle. He kicked and manhandled the youth who died three days later. Wheeler absconded while on bail and was never seen again. Cyclone Jack claims that he was caught by blacks and "dealt with". (No. 2 Crown Brief. CCT/N31. JUS. QSA)

"They must all suffer"

18. On 17 October 1858 Lieutenant Frederick Wheeler wrote his report to his commanding officer, Lieutenant John Murray, detailing his patrol of the Mount Larcom area.
19. Minutes of Evidence: 1861 Select Committee, pp.16–17.
20. Ibid. pp.17–18.
21. *Courier*, 25 July 1861. Author's italics.
22. Minutes of Evidence: 1861 Select Committee, pp.2–3.
23. *Courier*, 25 July 1861.
24. Minutes of Evidence: 1861 Select Committee, p.3.
25. Ibid. p.64.
26. Ibid. p.70.
27. Ibid. p.12.
28. *Moreton Bay Courier*, 7 May 1861.
29. *Courier*, 25 July 1861.
30. *Courier*, 31 July 1861.
31. Ibid.
32. Minutes of Evidence: 1861 Select Committee, p.18.
33. Ibid. p.13.
34. H.J. Lamond, *Native Mounted Police.*
35. Ibid. p.73.
36. Dundalli was hanged in Queen Street at the spot where the General Post Office now stands. Another Aborigine, known as Davey, was also hanged on that spot, on 22 August 1852. (The first Aborigines to be hanged in Brisbane were two alleged murderers, Merridio and Neugavil. On 31 July 1841, they were hanged on the cross-arm of the Tower Mill — now

known as the Brisbane Observatory Tower. See Arthur Laurie, *The Black War in Queensland*, read before the Meeting of the Royal History Society of Queensland, 23 October 1958).

37. At dawn on 27 October 1857, Hornet Bank Station was attacked by members of the Jiman tribe. When the blacks finally withdrew, eleven people lay dead or dying.
38. Letter, Woods/Colonial Secretary 12 March 1862. Author's italics. (Woods learned this first-hand through his conversations with Lieutenant Nicoll; also, he was told by men who worked in the district. Courtesy Gordon Reid, *A Nest of Hornets*.)
39. Ibid. Author's italics.
40. Gordon Reid, *A Nest of Hornets*.
41. Letter from Ross to Denison, 28 September 1857.
42. Letter from Lieutenant Murray to stockholders, 23 December 1857.
43. Scott and Thompson/Lieutenant Murray, 27 December 1857.

"I ran like hell!"

44. The "blacktrackers" Jack refers to are the native troopers. It was customary for officers to carry swords on patrol; the troopers refused to carry them as they were "too heavy".
45. An account of this massacre is given in A.L. Haydon's *Trooper Police of Australia*, Andrew Melrose, London, 1911 p.911.
46. Ibid. p.371.
47. *Advance Australia: an account of eight years' work, wandering and amusement in Queensland, New South Wales and Victoria,* Allen & Co., London, 1885.
48. E. Foreman, *The History and Adventures of a Queensland Pioneer*, Exchange Printing, Brisbane, 1928.
49. *Special journal to mark the Centenary of Queensland, 1859–69*, vol.VI, no.1. (In Minutes of Evidence: 1861 Select Committee, p.19, it is stated that the Manager of Kilcoy Station, Evan MacKenzie, was nicknamed "strychnine" by the blacks.)
50. A.L. Haydon, *The Trooper Police of Australia*, p.299.
51. Ibid.
52. G. Carrington, *Colonial Adventures and Experiences by a University Man*, AIAS, Canberra, 1871, p.80.
53. R.H. Mathews, *The Wombya Organisation of Australian Aborigines.*
54. A.L. Haydon, *The Trooper Police of Australia.*
55. Constance Petrie, *Tom Petrie's Reminiscences.*
56. Ibid.

57. Ibid.
58. Ibid.

"Gib me dat tin-opener"

59. A built-up mound of earth which forms the walls of a "dam" from which water is gravity-fed through pipes down to cattle troughs. In some instances, these troughs could be located miles away from the turkey nest.
60. "Bungi" is a word which, roughly translated, means, "my friend who is my junior".
61. Ear.

"He shot him through the head"

62. NSW Government Gazette, 1853, 1:655.
63. Letter from Bligh to Marshall, 13 February 1855.
64. *Wide Bay Chronicle*, 28 February 1861.
65. *Moreton Bay Courier*, 2 April 1861.
66. *Moreton Bay Courier*, 25 April 1861.
67. Report of the Northern Protector of Aborigines for 1902. QVP, 11, 1903, p.460.
68. Report of the Northern Protector of Aborigines for 1903, QVP, 1904, p.871.
69. *Rockhampton Chronicle*, 2 February 1861.
70. Editorial. *Courier*, 6 July 1861.
71. *Maryborough Chronicle*, 4 April 1861. (Reprinted from *Moreton Bay Courier*, 19 March 1861.)
72. Minutes of Evidence: 1861 Select Committee, p.147.
73. Ibid. p.145.
74. Report of the Select Committee, p.4. Lieutenant Rudolph Morisset's report regarding the blacks attacking him was, almost certainly, an untruth as the blacks referred to were quiet station blacks in the employ of the Mortimer brothers. It is a reasonable assumption that the troopers, realising that Morisset was unfamiliar with the situation, took the opportunity and slaughtered the members of an opposing tribe.

75. Ibid. p.6.
76. Ibid. p.33.
77. It is a pretty fair bet that Gulliver was shot by Lieutenant Powell or the troopers. According to reliable evidence, Gulliver was handcuffed and too drunk to walk properly, which tends to rule out the story that he *ran away* and escaped. On the other hand, he may have gammoned that he was drunk and his mates (Gulliver was an ex-trooper) may have helped him escape. No one can really say with certainty what happened, hence the mystery.
78. On 11 September 1847 three timber workers, James Smith, William Boller and William Waller, were working near the Pine River when attacked by blacks led by Dundalli. Boller and Waller died and Smith recovered.
79. Constance Petrie, *Tom Petrie's Reminiscences*.
80. Letter to Colonial Secretary, 20 December 1854, NSWVP, p.871.
81. Report of the Board of Inquiry, 1855, NSWVP, p.871.
82. NSWVP, 19 January 1855, p.874.
83. Registrar of Births, Deaths and Marriages, Brisbane.
84. Michael Terry, *War of the Warramullas*, Adelaide, Rigby, 1974.